AF483525

WHO'S TO KNOW
The Life and Times of a Grateful Life

Design by Sarah Meiers, production by Heather Shaw
of Mission Point Press.

ISBN: 979-8-3302-8400-9

Printed in the United States of America

WHO'S TO KNOW

The Life and Times of a Grateful Life

By Jon A. Hisey

TO FATE: The supposed force or power that predetermines events. The results of consequences.

TO LUCK: The chance happening of fortunate events, prosperity and success.

TO CAROL: My life's partner through it all, who was always there with patience, love, and an enormous gift of memory. I couldn't have done it, or this, or that without her.

TO MY CHILDREN: Joan Carol, Jon Clark, Jenifer Ann, and Jessica Louise, who enriched my life beyond measure with their love, laughter, and friendship.

TO MY GRANDCHILDREN: Julia Grace, Jon Andrew, Jenica Rose, Clarke Daniel, Claire Joan, Jenevieve Grace, Charles Jon, and Jaydee Louise. Our family and my world is a better place because of them.

TO THE ONES THAT JOINED MY WALK I AM THANKFUL: some just a few steps, some for miles, hundreds of inspirational characters and those that guided me with encouragement at critical crossroads.

TO THE DIRT AND DUST OF MY LONG-GONE UNKNOWN ANCESTORS. Thank you.

TO MY DESCENDANTS: I hope that someday some of you can write your own life's history.

Each of our lives is guided by fate and luck. We are shaped and influenced by current events and the significant historical benchmarks of our lives, be they personal, local, national, or global. A person's history within history. The events I included here are all true, culled from boxes of mementos, diaries, business records, ship's logs, photographs, and Carol's extensive travel journals. It's amazing all the things remembered, even past conversations from decades ago. How the contemporary history of our time ultimately filters down to each of our biographies. As to the quotes within the text, some are indelibly imprinted within my hippocampus, and some have been reconstructed or enhanced from a combination of recall and a little imagination of a long-ago moment. However, I can assure you that my attempt at accuracy was thoughtful and honest. This was my life; this was my voice.

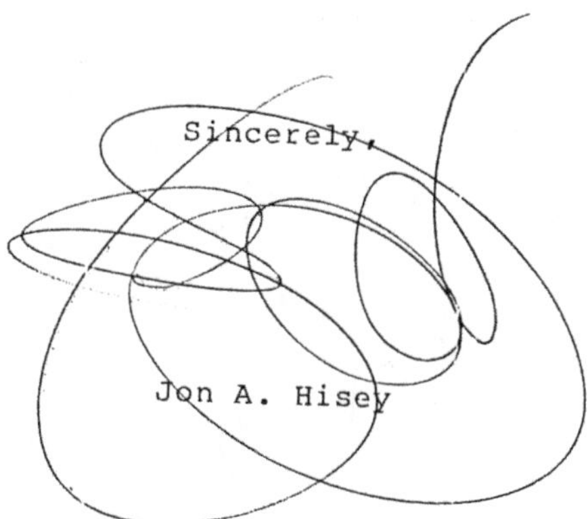

CONTENTS

PROLOGUE

SOMETIME IN MY MID-FORTIES TO EARLY FIFTIES, with a predisposition to history and biography, and an amount of introspection, I came up with an idea to write a letter to my grandchildren and their children's children. In that letter I was going to tell them who I was, what I did, what I thought, and attempt to opine on some words of wisdom from a descendant that they or their children's children will never know, and to shed a tiny light on ancestors of the nameless past. Sitting by the fire, singing their histories, dancing by the light of the moon, worshiping a rock, or stars, or a weeping willow by the river's edge. Mourning a loss, curious, asking why?

I have often wondered what my grandparents, much less great or great-great grandparents were like. Were they farmers? Were they educated? Merchants or mercenaries? Were they jailers or jailed? What did they do or think? I mean, really, if it were not for them, I would not be here.

We are all but a fragile long thread of mutual DNA. Just think, only five or six generations ago, you needed a spark to see in the dark.

I thought how precious it would have been to get a letter from one of my ancestors. I shared that idea with my wife, Carol, and a few friends, and they all thought it was worth pursuing. Well, it's 2020, and I'm still thinking about it, but now there seems an added sense of urgency. Several events have occurred since the seed was germinated in the back of my brain; parents died, friends and peers are passing away at an alarming rate, and I have become an old man whose shadow grows a little longer by the day. In 2020, 2021, and counting, COVID-19, a coronavirus, hit the United States and the world. We were in lockdown, no public dining in restaurants or personal gatherings, and masks were worn whenever we ventured out of our homes. Fear ruled the globe, and over one million and counting U.S. citizens died and it's estimated 30 million will perish worldwide.

Now the heavy scale of yesterdays far outweighs the light side of tomorrows, and while the fear of death has subsided, the fear of being forgotten has increased. It is my belief that there is continuity between each of us and the past as the growing chasm of time between my life and yours widens. Our own personal stories are important and can be meaningful to our curious descendants. Our lives are a tangled string of circumstances of who, what, when, where and whys.

The following is just a fragment of my feeble attempt to connect my time here with your time there. Pieces of events and moments of reflection were coaxed from one memory while thinking of another. My thoughts, actions, delights, and despair of a life born into the middle of the 20th century, a product of my time. It kind of got out of hand. But with the provenance of my ancestors (mostly from the northwestern and eastern European regions of the old world) and an innate sense of curiosity of the multiple mysteries of being human, I began to write, with history on my mind. A bit corny in places and a little vanity sneaks in sometimes without knocking. Fate was kind to me and luck was on my side, with gifts of unexpected opportunities. I was just an average man with an average intellect that lived an above-average life.

Although I was never asked to speak of myself and I never raised my hand for a chance, I reflected on the certainty of my past and pondered the uncertainty of the future. I began to write; anyone can write, so I did. Informative for the curious, perhaps a bit entertaining for a few. I tried to assemble these few moments of my life together in chronological order, but it quickly became a bit more complicated than expected so there is some hopscotch and leapfrogging along the way.

I can only hope that this task's worth to me will simply be when a distant grandchild amongst a group discussing family history will say, "Of course I never knew him … but I do know him."

This obviously evolved into more than a letter. Patience may be required.

THE EARLY DAYS

WITH EXCEPTIONS, 1944 WAS A GOD-AWFUL YEAR in the course of human history. The USA had a population of nearly 140 million. Franklin D. Roosevelt was president, and Henry Wallace was vice president. There were several hundred Civil War veterans, or their widows, who were still collecting disability benefits from the federal government.

In the spring of 1944, the world was in the midst of a war that would ultimately claim close to 80 million casualties including famine and disease plus untold wounded and displaced persons. American and Russian soldiers were about to discover Germany's Nazi concentration camps and the industrialized killing of over six million European Jews and "Misfits." Crematorium ovens and mass graves of the nameless marked the devil's evil. It would become the bloodiest century in all of human history.

Hideous, ideological, extremism and fanaticism is the fuel of hell.

Many Americans were tending their small victory gardens of summer vegetables and herbs to help the war effort. And citizens of color couldn't sit at a diner in some parts of America and order a cola, or even drink water from a public fountain.

Over 75,000 young US soldiers were waiting in England while US Generals Marshall and Eisenhower and our Allies were finalizing plans to invade Europe through Normandy on the northern coast of France to retake Europe and begin the ending of World War II. General MacArthur began his quest to retake the Pacific Islands after he and his family were "sneaked away" from Corregidor Island in March of 1942. He proclaimed his promise to the people of the Philippines that "I Shall Return."

Detroit's renowned manufacturing base and its suburbs was called "the cradle of democracy" producing more airplanes, tanks, Jeeps, and other war-related items than any other area in the country. In the middle of May in 1944, sugar, leather, gasoline, chocolate, and many other civilian goods were rationed and in short supply. A loaf of bread at the corner market would cost a dime. A gallon of gas was 22 cents and was pumped by an attendant in overalls. And a letter could be mailed first class for only three cents. On Thursday, May 18, 1944, the Tigers beat Philadelphia 1-0 and the stock market DJIA closed at a whopping 139.20. On the third floor of Women's Hospital in Detroit, Michigan, Jon Arthur Hisey was spanked into this world by Dr. Daniels at 11:30 a.m. A war baby. A generation that transformed American culture—the way we think, the way we communicate, and the way we pray.

*   *   *

I was raised by my parents, Beverly Grace Simpson Hisey and James Huffman Hisey in Wayne, Michigan, at 35645 Park Street, between two main east/west streets and a short walk to "downtown." Both parents were graduates of Michigan State College, (it became a university in 1955.) Hardwood trees lined the streets and sidewalks and houses had front porches. A typical small Americana town of about 6,000, located halfway between Detroit and Ann Arbor. It was officially established in 1869 on what was then called the Chicago Trail, just a worn Indian path which later became a stagecoach and then a train stop between Detroit and Chicago. Abandoned trolley tracks for streetcars were still embedded into the cement of Michigan Avenue.

On October 4, 1947, Army Air Force test pilot Captain Chuck Yeager made his way down a ladder into the open bomb bay doors of a World War II B-29 bomber while nursing two cracked ribs from a horseback riding accident the day before. He settled into the frigid, cramped seat at 20,000 feet of an X1 experimental rocket engine airplane that was hanging by a single bomb shackle. He locked the plane's door shut with the help of a ten-inch piece of sawed-off broomstick and was dropped into thin air. He fell a thousand feet before igniting the rocket engine and pointed her straight up to an altitude of 45,000 feet to become the first man to break the so-called "unbreakable" sound barrier, changing the future of aviation history forever. This anecdote would eventually help cement my enthusiasm and lifelong interest in aviation and early space exploration. My mother gave me a 1986 signed copy of Chuck Yeager's autobiography where he wished me a happy birthday.

Around 1917 my grandparents, Lois Huffman Hisey and Ventry Ross Hisey bought Wayne's local newspaper. In the early '30s they divorced, and V. Ross made his way down to Miami, Florida. He remarried and eventually, with a partner, built and operated a small-gauge railroad train in Camden Park, Key Biscayne Bay near Miami. He died there in 1959. Lois changed the name of the newspaper to *The Wayne Dispatch* and continued to publish it until my father, James Hisey, born August 23, 1919, on Sophia Street in Wayne, took it over in the early fifties.

I grew up reading biographies of American historical figures. I was drawn to the small details of history's back stories of early influential people, such as Daniel Boone, Kit Carson, Buffalo Bill (William Cody), Bill Hickok, Ben Franklin (waste not – want not) all the early presidents, several of Lincoln, Thomas Edison, and Henry Ford to name just a few. My heroes. The only fiction book that comes to mind is the *The Boxcar Children*, a story of orphan youngsters trying to stay together while living in an abandoned railroad boxcar. Later in life my heroes morphed into contemporary rocket jockeys.

I was baptized with uncertainty and skepticism at an early age.

My first memory of one of life's inevitable traumatic events came in the spring of 1950. I don't remember any arguments, no screaming or throwing dishes, just an image of the back of my dad stepping off the small wooden back porch onto the narrow cement walkway that led to the garage, with a big brown envelope under his arm, and a suitcase in his hand, and my mother grabbing my shoulder to lead me back into the kitchen, and hearing the spring-loaded screen door slamming shut between the past and my family's unknown future. He didn't stop or turn back or even wave; he just kept his pace. He left, leaving behind my mom, older brother James (Jim) and two-year-old brother Jerrold (Jerry) and me. Left to our own consequences. A casualty of secret conversations. Did he leave a scar from an unseen cut that can only heal from within? Was it painful with pain or just a lingering ache? I often wondered.

* * *

My mother and father were married on April 4, 1942, and divorced on April 19, 1952. Dad remarried on October 18, 1952, to Darleen Williams in her hometown of Charlevoix, Michigan. Mom had a few boyfriends, but never remarried.

In the mid-1950s when weather kept us inside after school, we watched a small 9-inch, 3-channel grainy black and white television screen in a large furniture box. It was considered to be the golden age of capitalism. It was boosted with the end of World War II and the "forgotten" 1950 Korean War that never ended, just a cease-fire agreement along the 38th parallel that still exists.

President Eisenhower served two terms of peace and prosperity, and in October 1952, Queen Elizabeth II began her reign and is still at it as I write this. [Editor's note: The Queen passed away on September 8, 2022.] In 1953 DNA and the double helix was discovered.

Eleven-year-old Jon.

I was raised within a quiet generation of typical Midwest culture. There was never talk of religion, politics, sex, or death. No "atta boys," hugs, "I love you," or displays of public affection. From an early age, it seems like I was always trying to sell something, whether it was lemonade or Kool-Aid on a street corner or collecting or trading baseball cards and marbles. I sold garden seeds door-to-door. It involved getting orders from customers, collecting the money, and delivering the vegetable and flower seeds. In the spring, I was paid with incentive awards chosen from a small catalog.

In the summer of 1955, I built a three-level tree house out of salvage lumber in a nice maple tree in the front yard between the sidewalk and the street. I was quite proud of it. Sometimes my mom would put my lunch or dinner in a bucket, and I would pull it up with a rope. Unfortunately, after about a long month the city manager and my dad came to see me and gently convinced me to remove it because it was on the city easement and the neighbors were complaining. So down it came. This was about the same summer Dad and Darleen took us, the three boys, north to Charlevoix, Michigan, to meet our new step grandparents, Rowley and Florence Williams on the corner of Ferry and Black roads. They were very nice people who lived in a big house with one bathroom. It was a working farm with cows, chickens, pigs, and a large vegetable garden, tractor rides and had a functioning outhouse between the barn and chicken coop. We continued to go up there each summer for a week until Jim and I entered high school.

Shortly after Dad left, Mom rented out two of the three bedrooms upstairs to single ladies who wore white girdles with clasps that held up nylon stockings with a dark line down the back that they always fiddled with at the top of the stairs where the big mirror was.

We weren't poor—we just didn't have any money. I didn't know it at the time, but Grandpa (Arthur Leon) and Grandma (Augusta) Simpson regularly helped support Mom throughout her life. Even after Grandma died, Mom still received small quarterly checks from a trust that Grandpa started in the 1930s.

It was also during this time frame that I started to collect newspapers. I would bundle them with sisal twine and store them on one side of our garage. More than once I had accumulated tons of newspapers with stacks as high as I could reach with only small walkways in and around the garage. Dad would come over to help me load up a trailer and take them to the recycle yard next to the railroad tracks to get weighed and collect some spending money. Dad was no hero of mine—mine were in history books. He was not a stranger, or live in. He was always in the periphery, standing in the wings, rarely center stage. In reflection I would say enigma might describe him best … maybe he was yearning for a family that could not exist. It wasn't like we were joined at the hip (like some father and sons are), it was more like we were in different rooms, even if we were sitting together having lunch. Did he love me? Yes. Did I love him? Yes.

I had a habit of burying money in various locations in the backyard between the garage and the stone fence that separated our yard from the alley. I also stashed money under the small wooden back porch and in the crawl space under the back room and behind the baseboard in my bedroom's small closet. Some of that loot might still be there.

Our home on Park Street was a small 1,750-square-foot, two-story house with three bedrooms and one bathroom all on the second floor. There was an extra room over a crawl space with a half bath. It had a full basement with a huge oil-burning furnace that sat right in the middle. A quarter section of the basement had shelving for Dad's model train tracks and an unpainted wood workbench and a half can of paint that he had left, empty of trains and tracks and tools to repair things with. They were all gone too.

It was a good neighborhood. There was a core group of 9 or 10 of us, a mix of girls and boys of similar age. In the summer we would be outside all day and even after dinner and into the night. Most of the time our house and yard would be the center of all the action, and where we would congregate and form our games or mischief of the day or night. My brothers and I had little or no supervision. After the divorce, Mom had to work during the day. She took the bus to Dearborn and sometimes worked the dinner shift at Temples dining room, an upscale tablecloth restaurant on South Wayne Rd.

The space race between the USA and Soviet Union began in the fall of 1957 when NASA introduced its original seven astronauts. Space exploration by humans fascinated me from the beginning and was a lifelong hobby of interest.

It was the winter of 1957–58 that Dad introduced us boys to snow skiing. We would take the 6- or 7-hour road trip to Charlevoix and the next morning drive over to Hidden Valley Ski Resort near Gaylord, Michigan. He arranged to trade advertising in the *Dispatch* newspaper for our lift tickets. It became a life-long sport for me and future family that I have enjoyed into my mid-seventies.

Once I discovered fireworks at about 12 or 13 years of age, a match was set to a fuse of trouble. My friends Gary and Larry Houston would go to Arkansas for a few weeks in the summer to see family. I would give them money to buy "real" cherry bombs,

M-80 blockbusters, and TNTs. Most had waterproof fuses, and all were outlawed in the state of Michigan. We would place them in mailboxes and downspouts, then hide nearby to watch the destructive explosion. I can remember dropping a couple blockbusters into the storm sewer and the water would shoot several feet into the air. They were really loud and dangerous. One night in the middle of our mischief the Wayne Police started to chase us, so we split up. I was running through yards, hopping fences, and eventually finding my way home to safety in my bedroom. After a few minutes my mother called up to me, "Jon! Come down here! The police are here!" I confessed and was given a stern, serious warning. Then one of the two policemen marched me up to my bedroom where I had to give up the rest of my fireworks stockpile (except a few in the bottom of a drawer I had innocently forgotten about). One time, on Devil's Night, we collected a volunteer's poop and put it in a brown paper bag, then placed it on a grumpy neighbor's front porch. We then lit the bag on fire and rang the doorbell, then hid across the street behind some shrubs and watched him stomp out the fire with his feet. That was fun! It seems terribly mean now. No boundaries.

It felt like I was on my own; there never seemed to be an anchor or a sense of stability. Mom did her best to raise three boys, and as I look back from those distant years, I can appreciate her struggles with pride. I loved my grandfather and grandmother Simpson. They were important to me at a young age and my grandmother became a grounding influence to me and to my own young family until she died in May 1977. My father's mother, Grandmother Lois, remarried later in life to widowed Harold Dietrich, past Mayor of Wayne and owner of the local Buick dealership. She was a kind lady but somewhat distant. Grandpa Hisey lived in Coral Gables, Florida, and I vaguely remember meeting him on two or three occasions.

Although baptized in the Methodist church, at an early age there seemed to be no core belief, no religion at home except an occasional church outing and a perfunctory grace before Christmas and Easter dinners. I don't recall any conversation about rights or wrongs, the birds and the bees, or family histories. As a youngster I must have formulated my beliefs, values, and work ethics by listening to somebody, someone, sometime, and maybe a little help from ancestral DNA.

Another vivid memory of childhood was standing over the dining room heat register that was directly over the old and loud oil-burning furnace, for what seemed like hours into the night with a souvenir Indian tomahawk in my hand while waiting for my mother to get home from waiting tables. If I heard a noise somewhere I would go to investigate it with my weapon, cautiously looking behind the door that led to the basement and rechecking that all windows and doors were latched and locked on the first floor before returning to my warm perch in the dining room while my two brothers slept. As soon as I heard my mother's approach I would disappear into my bed.

For two summers I played Little League baseball. I was always the smallest and slowest member of the team, a left-handed relief pitcher who rarely had a chance to play. I was ambidextrous and played all sports—except golf—as a lefty. I wrote and ate right-handed. Our team's pitcher became a professional ball player for the Detroit Tigers farm team and eventually became a coach. One fall I played halfback on a junior football league with my brother Jim; as usual I was the smallest member of the group and can remember the one time running with the football and somehow scoring a touchdown (it was probably fixed). I also took trumpet lessons for two years and was a Cub Scout.

* * *

I do know everything changed on December 18, 1956, the day Grandpa Simpson died. Our history together was fixed: a used smoking pipe and leather tobacco pouch, a wooden handle letter opener, that I still use, and a soiled handsaw that hangs in my garage. I believe that event in my life triggered the end of my childhood. I began to realize then that there can be no certainty in an uncertain world. Not in religion or health, family, or friends, and not in life itself. It marked by default, when I became the one that mowed the lawn, raked the leaves, ran to the small Sunshine Market across Michigan Avenue to pick up a quart of milk and a stick of butter ten minutes before dinner and put my name to the running tab.

That summer my brothers and I moved to Grandma's house, a wonderful house in an upscale neighborhood in Redford, called Rosedale, just two blocks from Grand River Blvd. and a short bus ride to downtown Detroit. Mom would come and go as needed. Over the years a frequent recurring memory of meaningful moments that summer would wander back into my thoughts.

Often in the late afternoon, when the sun was west, and it was quiet, I found myself on the front screened-in porch sitting in one of the two big heavy rocker chairs alone with Grandma. We would be quiet, sometimes with fresh lemonade made with lemons from the fruit and vegetable wagon that came through the neighborhood on a weekly basis. Rocking, peaceful, thinking our thoughts, listening to the faint sounds of nature and the neighborhood, she a new widow, me without my grandpa, but feeling safe, with only the coo … coo … coo of the dove. Somehow, I knew it was going to be all right. The priceless gift of the dove, the soft coo of the dove always brings me home to the calm of peace and unspoken love.

After we returned to Wayne that fall from Grandma Simpson's, I started delivering the *Detroit News* in the afternoon. My route had over 40 customers and was basically in my surrounding neighborhood. I would trifold the papers and tuck them in my newspaper bag that stretched between the handlebars of my bike, ready to be thrown onto my customers' front porches or yards or bushes. I remember one particular dark early wintry Sunday morning (Sunday papers were delivered in the morning). It had snowed during the night but there was still a light snowfall that sparkled under the streetlights. I stopped at the local Chum's donut shop and bought a hot glazed donut. It was hard peddling and steering through the snow, alone, cold to the bone, struggling with every forward move. It took a few hours to complete my route. I vividly remember that special morning of solitude and cold and working it through daybreak, being aware and embracing the quiet beauty of nature's moment of peacefulness. Was I frustrated, angry, or in agony? No … exhilarated. From about that age, I have usually read a newspaper or two most every day of my life.

* * *

I attended sixth, seventh, and eighth grades at West Side Junior High School. It was previously Wayne's High School where my father graduated in 1937 and was conveniently located just one block west of our house at the end of Park Street.

One day during Mr. Dent's seventh grade social studies class, the students were exceptionally rowdy and noisy. Frustrated, Mr. Dent finally shouted out, "Listen class I've had enough! All I want to hear is silence!" So … after a few quiet moments I remarked for all to hear, "S-i-l-e-n-c-e." Before I knew it, I was dragged out of the classroom by the back of my neck, down the hall and into the principal's office, where he proceeded to reach for an oversized paddle and wacked my bum several times.

During the fall in the eighth grade, I was standing alone next to the gym's wall at a school dance, when a classmate briefly introduced me to a girl named Carol Clark. She was a little taller than I was at the time. I stayed put and don't remember saying a word other than "hi," before Carol returned to the dance floor without me.

The lower branch of the Rouge River flowed from west to east right through the City of Wayne, on the north side of Michigan Avenue and was crossed by three automobile bridges and one train trestle. The river meandered toward Dearborn past the Henry Ford Estate of Fairlane, and eventually emptied into the Detroit River near the massive Ford Motor Rouge Assembly Plant.

The river was important to me, a refuge of sorts as a young boy and into adolescence. The Rouge was only three blocks from our front porch, an easy walk north on Clark Street (which coincidentally ended at our driveway) and across the four-lane Michigan Avenue. Clark Street stopped with a steel barrier at the top of a bluff. There was a steep, small, narrow overgrown trail that led down to the river, and from there I would walk several hundred feet along the shore following a horseshoe bend back toward the southwest and the C & O railroad bridge on the west side of town. Just after the bend there was a place along the riverbank that flooded every spring.

In the summer I would step down through scrub and brush to the water's edge where I would often day camp, always alone. If you didn't know what you were looking for, you would walk right past it, and if you were quiet and laid low while pressing yourself up against the damp earthen bank, no one would see you. It was great, and it was safe with long grass that was soft and always laid flat from the river's spring current. I would make a small fire pit each summer with rocks and river mud and kept a small cache of dry firewood and kindling that was always ready nearby. It was quiet, only the fire's crackle and the soft babbling sounds of the river's current against the shore's resistance. A can of Van Camp pork and beans and a hot dog over a fire and bottle of Uptown soda pop from Sunshine Market made a perfect meal. I would take the point of my scout opener and walk it along the can's top, bending back the lid for a handle and set it on the flat stone positioned next to the fire. Then I pierced the skin of the hot dog with the point of a stick that I fashioned from a young tree branch and held it over the coals until it was almost burnt. It didn't take long before the sense of contentment prevailed. It was my secret spot.

While remembering moments and events in an attempt to organize my life's journey I have come to realize how important water was to me. Could it be the little spot next to the river was the source of my lifelong attraction to it? To play in it, to swim in it, to snorkel and dive into it, to sail and cruise and paddle in it, to ski on it, and float on it, to live next to it, to smell it, taste it, and to love it and revere it. Maybe a panacea?

*   *   *

One time, soon after earning my first BB gun, I was in the backyard just fooling around, shooting at tin cans. There was a tall evergreen hedge that you could peek through between our yard and Mr. and Mrs. Chisholm's next door. On this bright summer day Mrs. Chisholm was hosting a luncheon for one of the ladies' civic clubs of Wayne. Tables were set up in their backyard, covered with white cloth, and real dishes and silverware, and she served tea, champagne, and fancy sandwiches that had no crust.

A big black crow happened to be flying over my head and without thinking I pointed my gun at the moving target and fired. I had never killed anything and obviously had no chance to hit a moving target 30 to 40 feet away. But I did hit it, and the wounded bird came smashing down into Chisholm's backyard between tables, squealing wildly as it was flapping its one good wing in the middle of screaming women as they scrambled, spilling as they fumbled and stumbled to avoid being hit by the delirious intruder. Soon I saw Mr. Chisholm come running out of the garage with a shovel to finish the poor creature off. Needless to say, I did not stick around much longer. After a few hours away from the scene, I pieced together what I saw and what my mother told me after she listened to Mr. Chisholm's angry report. She took my BB gun away … for a while.

One late spring, my friends and I found two empty 50-gallon drum barrels down by the river's shore. We fashioned a raft by using some small logs of river drift and tied everything together with some twine. Since it was my idea, it was decided that I would try it first. It was not my nature to go first in anything. I hopped on with a long pole we made from a tree to push with and to balance myself. I don't think I made it 10 feet from shore before losing my balance and dumping into the river. Scrambling up the muddy bank we all watched the barrels separate and float with the current down the "mighty" Rouge.

Occasionally my friends and I went down to the river at the end of Clark St. with our BB guns, to play cowboys and Indians. We would shoot at each other while we ran around and hid behind trees with a standing rule that there would be no shooting above the belt. One time as I crouched down and poked my head out from a tree, I was hit in my right eye. Dropping to the ground screaming, with my hand tight against my eye, my panicked friends guided me home. My mother borrowed a car and rushed me to the emergency room at Eloise County Hospital at the corner of Merriman and Michigan Avenue. When the doctor removed the BB from my eyelid, he told us that I was lucky, and that if I was hit just a tiny fraction above where it lodged, I probably would have been blind in that eye. My mother took my gun away again … for a while.

In 1958, my friend Steve Tatro and I started a lawn mowing "business." At first, we had to use our hand push mowers, but by the middle of summer we were able to invest in a new, bright green, gas-powered Lawnboy. At the end of the season Steve bought a new Vespa motor scooter with his money. I hid mine.

Next to the Clarence Bell Ford dealership on Michigan Avenue across from Wayne's old graveyard there was a bowling alley. They had recently converted the manual pin placement workers with automatic machines, except one person that could manage all eight lanes. On two occasions my friends and I sneaked into the back door of the bowling alley. As soon as you stepped in, there was a long walkway to the left and right that allowed the monitor to access and fix any problems that might crop up. It was very noisy as the automatic setting machines rumbled and tumbled to the rhythms of metal clinking. We watched the care-taker as he sat in a wooden chair that was tipped back against the wall with his feet resting on the corner of a machine and his arms folded, nestled on the bulge of his stomach like he was taking a nap, oblivious to noise. After deciding that the coast was clear, we made a dash to the pins that were moving within the machine, grabbed a few and made our getaway within a few seconds. We climbed up on the roof with the attached metal ladder and threw them off the front side of the building in an effort to get them over the road and into the old cemetery. Crazy fun, insanely stupid.

The second and last time we did this, as we were climbing down the ladder, we spotted a slow-moving police car without lights approaching toward us from the dark alley. We all sepa-rated and started to run. I made it to a nearby house on Elizabeth Street and was hiding in the bushes waiting for the coast to clear, when I started to see a flashlight waving back and forth coming toward me. As soon as I heard footsteps quicken, I made a dash for it with enough adrenalin to break a four-minute mile. I can still remember feeling the policeman's hand on my back as he tried to grab me as I started to run, and heard him yell, "Come on Jonny, I know it's you!"

The next day my dad picked me up at the house and drove me to the police station where the decorated uniformed police chief, a friend of my dad's and warden of the town jail, gave me a convincing lecture while we stood in the middle of a small, faint green cement cell. They gave me a forceful warning. This event pretty much ended my wayward days of delinquency. For a while.

There were episodes of miscellaneous misdemeanors of incidental shoplifting, smoking, a few beers, "borrowing" a shop truck a few times from a local plumber for joy riding, stealing batteries from cars as needed, damaging mailboxes and gutters on private property with my annual supply of cherry bombs and M-80 firecrackers, or wayward pumpkins thrown from a car. No boundaries.

Our house had one bathroom upstairs; it was small with a sloped ceiling that followed the roof line. A small double hung window with a pleated sheer lined curtain covered the bottom half of the window that you had to lift off to open for some fresh air. There was light yellow cracked linoleum on the floor with an old-fashioned "ball and claw" stained cast iron tub. No shower or curtain around the tub. A few times during the night if you looked out my bedroom window across the alleyway and turned your gaze above our garage and into the neighbor's lighted upstairs apartment window, you would learn enough of the birds and bees to fill a textbook. Educational, to say the least.

Downstairs there was a spare bedroom with a toilet and tiny sink with an oak wood floor that always stunk, as you might imagine with three boys. There was no shower in the house, so as a young teenager, I built one in the basement. I attached a green garden hose to the standing washtub and fastened a sprayer to the other end and hung it from the ceiling with a nail and a wire fashioned from a coat hanger. I made a raised slatted wood platform from a found pallet to stand on that allowed water to find its way to the existing floor drain a few feet away. I hooked a shower curtain from the ceiling to keep the water from spraying all over the basement. But for real privacy it was better to shut the door that led down to the basement. It actually worked pretty well, except you had to turn the water on at the sink and hope that the hot and cold mix was almost right, and in the winter, it was really cold. Mom never used the darn thing.

During the Christmas holidays, I would do most of the shopping in Wayne or take a bus ride to Dearborn. And I wrapped everyone's presents, including my own.

In the summer of 1958, Mom took us (Jim, Jon, and Jerry) to Niagara Falls in our new Ford Fairlane car—the first car my mother ever bought. Niagara made quite a lasting impression on me, and I returned there several times with my own family. I became quite an authority on the geographical and hydro/industrial history of the falls and its many daredevils, including blindfolded tightrope walkers, and the men and women who perished going over the falls in an assortment of barrels or other manmade devices by hubris mostly, and the ones who survived by luck mostly, intrigued me. I took Carol and our two young children, Joan and Jon, for several years to the museums to see and feel up close the wet tourist attractions. I eventually designed a spherical contraption with two compressed air tanks, that would safely take me over the Horseshoe Falls and into history. Luckily, I never made it, much less tried.

Near the end of the 1950s there was a trampoline craze that swept the country and three local trampoline centers opened. The owners would install two rows of five or six trampolines level to the ground about four feet apart. My brother Jerry and I became quite adept at the new sport. We could do all the basic tricks, plus back flips, two rotations, and front flips. The one I liked best was to get as high as possible, straight up, then dive straight down with my arms spread out like a swan dive. The trick was to tuck your head in at the very last possible moment and land perfectly aligned on the back of your neck and shoulders, then bounce up and do a half twist with a sit down. Another fun thing to do that Jerry and I got good at was when (the tramp center wasn't very busy) we would start at the end, get as high as we could then jump several feet away onto the next trampoline. By the time we got 5 or 6 tramps down the row we were really high and out of control. We didn't do this often but when we did the manager would come out and start yelling at us to stop. Very dangerous but thrilling.

One time on a trip with Mom on the way to Florida we stopped at a motel in Tennessee that was next to a trampoline center. After a few minutes of Jerry and I doing our usual routine of tricks, a small crowd began to gather around to watch. We reveled in the oohs and aahs and a little applause. Shortly after that, the country's trampoline craze went bust; I assume it was because of too many accidents and lawsuits.

*　*　*

One summer my brother Jim and I teamed up with a father and son who were going up north to pick cherries near Traverse City. We packed some clothes, a little food and before dawn we were on our way, expecting to bunk up with some farm laborers and return in a week or two with pockets full of money. Eventually, we arrived near Traverse City and began to pull up to cherry farms to ask if they needed help with picking their crops. Each one gave us a variation of the word "no." So, after six or seven attempts, and the shadow of twilight looming, the father gave up and decided to head back to Wayne. This was before expressways had simplified and sped up travel between the Detroit area and Michigan's north country. Eventually, we arrived home early the next morning with less enthusiasm than when we started. And no money. Over the course of a few summers Mom would take us up to Houghton Lake to Mary and Norm Martin's cottage. Mary was Mom's best friend from the early days of Wayne. They remained lifelong friends. Mary had two boys, Jim who was three years older than I and Jon (no h) who was my brother Jim's age. We learned to water ski behind an aluminum boat with a small outboard engine.

In the fall of 1958, I started my freshman year at Wayne Memorial High School, on the corner of Glenwood and Fourth Street. Most of the time in my first year I had to walk about two miles to school, via a trail on the south side of the Rouge River between Elizabeth and Sims Street. During my first year in high school, I felt like the guy who, when playing musical chairs, and the music stopped, was always the one left awkwardly standing without a chair.

Near the end of the ninth grade, I was next to my locker after school was out, when Carol Clark came up to me and asked, "Jon, my brother is getting married in June, would you like to go to the wedding with me?" With fear on my face, I turned around without a word, slammed shut and locked my locker door and proceeded down the hall in a mix of a fast walk and a slow jog to the nearest school exit door. I have continually been reminded of how this clumsy encounter would be the start of our life together.

By the beginning of my sophomore year, my interest and comfort level with girls completely changed. There were two hayrides scheduled around Halloween that Fall when Carol tried again and asked me to go on my first hayride. I said, "Sure." I remember she said, "Really?" Later on that same day, I was asked by Marcia Giles to go on the next night's hayride. I said "Sure." She said, "Really?"

After a few dates with several other girls, my junior high school year ended with Carol and I spending more time together.

THE SIXTIES

TRANSFORMATIVE DAYS

AT THE BEGINNING OF THE 1960S, a gallon of gas and a gallon of milk cost about the same at 36 cents, and a loaf of Wonder bread only a quarter. You could buy a new 1964 Ford Mustang convertible for $2,650. On August 16, 1960, Air Force pilot Capt. Joe Kittinger became the first human to enter the void of space when he stepped off a tiny ledge of his balloon capsule at 102,800 feet above Earth to begin his ten-minute free fall parachute jump, reaching a speed of 614 mph. I was privileged to meet and talk to him later in life at an air show in Punta Gorda, Florida, and got his autograph.

The decade was filled with monumental changes. It seemed like Americans started to rethink or question everything: social norms, politics, sexuality, religion, civil rights, and inequality. Political assassinations, enormous internal opposition to the Vietnam War, riots in the streets, and the forced resignation of Richard Nixon after leaders of his own Republican Party had the courage to tell him impeachment was certain and that his presidency was over.

A country of confused citizens is a country in trouble. —JAH

On a positive level, the decade was filled with the United States's commitment to President Kennedy's goal, "before this decade is out, to land a man on the moon and return him safely to earth." NASA's last Mercury solo flight with Gordon Cooper was in 1963, followed by ten Gemini missions of two-person capsule flights, capped by the three-person *Apollo 12* mission in November 1969. The decade's last flight was the second landing on the moon.

As for me? My times of troubled delinquency slowly faded and dissolved into my past without a visit to court or a juvenile record. Luck, and perhaps some intervention of my family's network of local peers and ownership of one of the town's newspapers may have helped.

During 1960–61 my height went from five feet to a whopping six feet and my shoe size to 11½. Acne invaded my face and back and my weight was just over 100 pounds. In the spring of 1960, I came down with a severe case of mononucleosis. It was bad enough to require spending two weeks in Annapolis Hospital, where twice a day a nurse would come in and give me a shot in the rump and take some blood from my arm. Luckily, this was my only stay in a hospital (to date). Grandma Simpson came to help me convalesce at home for another few weeks by fixing my meals and monitoring the pills and schoolwork, except for my typing class.

My mom and dad both decided they should attend parent teacher conferences together that year. I'm sure it was a combination of not being a very good student and my missing a lot of school from the mono disease. When they met my typing teacher, they introduced themselves as the parents of Jon Hisey. The teacher gave them a quizzical look. She went "Hmmmm. What was that name again? Jon Hisey, he's in your third hour typing class." So, she pulled out the roster and said, "Oh yes! He's right here." Baffled … she whispered, "There is something odd going on here." After a few minutes they put two and two together and realized that I had title blocked all my work with the pseudonym Sinclair Bennett! They apparently all had a great laugh. My mom and dad both loved to tell that story. Maybe the teacher did too.

May 5, 1961, America's first astronaut Alan Shepard was launched into space for a quick 15-minute flight of fame and fortune from Cape Canaveral, Florida. After a four-hour wait lying on his back, waiting from an accumulation of various anomalies of the countdown, he peed in his spacesuit. Finally exasperated, his patience collecting in a puddle of urine, he radioed to NASA Flight Control. "Come on man—light this candle!" So they did and off he went enhancing my lifetime interest in America's space program and its astronauts. As an adult I collected several astronaut and space-related biographies, autobiographies, and autographs, including Shepard's.

*　*　*

At the start of my senior year, I was still struggling as a student. I was a confused, undisciplined adolescent when a few things happened on the way to adulthood that positively changed the trajectory of my life. Carol and I became more serious, and two teachers came into my world. Miss Barbara Dix, my young and pretty English teacher, introduced me to Ernest Hemingway, and several other twentieth-century American authors. She gave me the attention that I needed and encouraged me to read and write. I definitely had a crush on her and if there really is a teacher's pet, I was one. Most importantly, I met Timothy J. Dyer who taught government and history. This happened to be Mr. Dyer's first year of teaching. He was fresh out of Eastern Michigan University. Throughout my school years I had been a struggling C student who didn't take the responsibility of schoolwork seriously and was just a few steps away from becoming a chronic wayward delinquent. No paddle, no rudder, and no canoe.

Mr. Dyer, for some unknown reason, took me under his wing and nurtured me, trusted me, and encouraged me. He became my mentor. Luckily, I had always enjoyed history, social studies, and politics, and soon my grades began to come up in all my classes. By the middle of my senior year, I was a B+ student and Mr. Dyer started talking about the possibility of him helping me get accepted into college. He took Bill Coole (class president and super jock, an all-A student) and me to Washington, DC. He introduced us to our state representatives and senators, and we got to tour the Capitol buildings and all the Washington highlights. He seemed to have connections and it was a great experience. I have returned to Washington several times.

In the winter of 1961–62 he asked me to help him drive to Madison, Wisconsin, where he was attending a Catholic Newman Club Conference, as its president. I remember when we were on I-94 heading west at dusk in a snowstorm near New Buffalo, Michigan, when Mr. Dyer hit a spot of ice that caused the car to slide across the highway while doing two 360-degree revolutions to the opposite shoulder before he regained control. He quickly took the next exit and stopped at a gas station, where he got out of the car, knelt on a knee, and did a dozen Hail Marys before getting back into the car and finishing our trip. Mr. Dyer was active in the Catholic church his whole life. At the time he lived in Ypsilanti, one block from Eastern Michigan University, with his widowed aunt in an upstairs flat. He was a teacher who befriended me and gave me the chance at school that allowed me the self-awareness to make a much-needed course correction and eventually an extraordinary life. Because of him I am me. Fate.

Tim later became principal of Wayne High School, then superintendent of the Wayne-Westland school district. As superintendent, he mentioned me in his commencement speeches at the University of Michigan Chrysler Arena, when our two children Joan and Jon graduated from high school in 1981 and '82. He also became a doctor and regent for Eastern Michigan and a councilman and mayor of Ypsilanti before he left to become the superintendent of the Phoenix, Arizona, school district, at the time one of the nation's largest. He then moved to Washington, DC, where he led the National Association of Secondary School Principals. Sadly, he passed away on April 12, 2018. Regrettably I had lost touch with Tim for too many years before he died. It is good to occasionally reach out to your mentors.

Tim said, "Hate is an evil and destructive emotion. It ignores reason and intellectual inquiry and should be eradicated whenever it raises its ugly head. The only way to do this is through educated enlightenment. It is the most effective way to eliminate prejudice, ignorance, discrimination, and hate."

*　*　*

One summer I built a "kayak" made of wood struts joined at the bow and stern and covered with some kind of green canvas. Friends helped me load it into the 1949 red Ford convertible that Dad had kept in our garage. Each of us held a grip on the boat to keep it from turning into a kite as we drove to Newburg Lake on Hines Park Drive, near Plymouth. I was unanimously chosen—no surprise—to be the first one to try it out. After a few timid minutes of trying to balance myself, before I could even paddle, I realized that the water in the bottom of the kayak was increasing at an alarming rate before tipping over in about three feet of water. Forlorn, I walked back to shore, hanging on to a half-submerged kayak toward a laughing group of friends and strangers that had accumulated on shore.

In junior and senior years, my social confidence started to

climb, and I began to participate in several extracurricular activities. My circle of friends grew as I became a member of the Key Club, participated in a number of student activities and assemblies, and lettered on the varsity tennis team. I was also a member of the Thespians Club and was chosen for good roles in the two plays I auditioned for—Clarence in *Life with Father* and the Lion in *Wizard of Oz*. I was the coward, and Carol was the star while playing the lead part of Dorothy.

To call Carol on our black rotary dial phone I would first need to ask the mouthpiece, "Is anybody there?" Because it was a party line, more than one household was connected to it. It was not unusual for Carol and me to spend an hour talking before someone would break into our conversation and say, "Enough talk you two," or, "I need the line."

I also entered talent shows with my friends, impersonating the Kingston Trio, a popular folk ballad singing group of the time ("Hang Down Your Head Tom Dooley"). In my junior and senior years, I called myself the "Duke," but now I can't remember if anyone else called me that. I drove Dad's red 1949 Ford convertible as my own. When the solenoid starter broke, I rigged up an ordinary electrical light toggle switch under the dashboard and connected it to a typical round house doorbell that you pressed to start the car. This was the only time in my life that I understood what makes a car work.

✳ ✳ ✳

Carol and I graduated from Wayne Memorial High School somewhere in the middle of a class of over 425 students. It was the end of one of life's important chapters and the beginning of unknown unwritten chapters.

I think my years of public education and the extraordinary help and influence from Mr. Dyer and to some extent Miss Dix and

Jon Hisey, 1962

Carol Clark, 1962

the stability of Carol, provided me the tools to be able to greet my future. To leave the angst of adolescence and shed some of the insecurities of youth, I felt confident to pursue my goal of teaching American history, political science and geography in high school, while motorcycling through Europe in the summers. Carol had been accepted into Michigan's Olivet College to obtain her teaching degree in the field of elementary education.

The last boat I built had two plywood pontoons, caulked and painted bright blue and watertight. Carol, two friends, and I hauled it up to Woodland Lake near Brighton, Michigan, where Carol's parents had a small mobile home they used in the summer. It was stout and heavy and looked seaworthy. I had quite a bit of confidence in this one as we slid her into the lake. "It floated!" we all shouted as Carol and I grabbed the paddles and hopped on the two pontoons. "Finally," I said. "Finally, what?" Carol said. The lake was shallow for a few hundred feet before a big drop-off. We started with excitement and encouragement from onlookers at the beach. Carol's mom and dad were there too, although they seemed to be a bit quiet with doubt. As we headed out toward the deep water, the left pontoon where Carol was sitting started to get a little lower in the water, and before long she realized the inevitability of the situation and abandoned the ship and swam back to shore. Soon I began frantically paddling in reverse and eventually slid myself off into the shallows as the left side of the boat scraped along the lake's bottom. We dragged it back onto shore, let it drain, and took it back to Wayne. That would be my last attempt at any kind of boat building until the mid-1990s in Charlevoix, when I built a hydroplane from a kit that we christened *Goofy* after a Disney character. It worked great with a 15-hp Johnson outboard engine; it felt like you were going 100 miles an hour when you were probably moving along at 25.

* * *

What a difference a year can make … or a month, or even just a date can make a big difference in a life. Even just a moment, a word or bullet can change world history. Little did I know or expect, that I/we were about to be launched into maturity—missing, without knowing, some of the normal rites of passage. Our adolescent love was about to explode into fragments of uncertainty, fearless in our own innocence, starting our lives together on a high wire.

In the late afternoon of August 17, 1962, Carol Louise Clark and I were married at the Wayne Methodist Church by minister Cardwell Prout. It was a small, informal wedding, Dad and Darleen, Carol's parents, Grandma Simpson, and all our siblings were there. My mother was in the hospital for a gallbladder operation. We had a reception dinner at the Howard Johnson's on the corner of Belleville and Ecorse Rd. close to I-94. We each had the special of the day: hot turkey sandwich with mashed potatoes and gravy and green beans, $2.95 per.

From there, we began our honeymoon by driving across the Ambassador Bridge into Canada in Mom's 1962 Chevrolet Impala. After about an hour into Canada we stopped at a small motel to spend the night. The man at the desk asked if I was married—I looked about 15 years old at the time—and I said, "Yes, we just got married, we are on our honeymoon." He said, "Prove it." I went out to the car and got the certificate of marriage the minister gave us. I was 18 and Carol was 17, (2 weeks shy of 18). Our honeymoon destination was New York with a two-night stop at Niagara Falls, where we rented a tiny roadside cabin for about $3 a night. We then drove through New York to New York City, then to Atlantic City where we watched Bert Parks emcee the Miss America Pageant from cheap balcony seats.

That summer I started "Jon College Painting Co." to earn money for school. We printed some flyers and distributed them door-to-door in a few subdivisions, advertising bedrooms painted for $15 cash, with the customer buying the paint and supplies. While painting the exterior of a big white house in Wayne, I met Lou Singer, my customer's son. He told me he was going to start building his own house the next spring in Ann Arbor and asked if I wanted to help him. I said, "Sure, if I was available, I would be glad to." Lou and his wife were professors at the University of Michigan.

In the fall of 1962 Carol, Mom, Jerry, and Tim Dyer drove me up to Central Michigan University in Mt. Pleasant. It was an emotional event. My room number was 122 in Barnes Hall, where I shared a two-bedroom dormitory with 3 other freshmen. The bathrooms and showers were down the hall. That's all I can remember of my first year of college except for watching the "Cuban Missile Crisis" in October on a small black and white television in the Barnes Hall lounge. On most weekends

I hitchhiked back and forth to Wayne to be with Carol and family. For the return trip Carol would usually drop me off on Grand River Road in Brighton (before I-96 was built) and from there I would get a ride to Lansing and then another ride to Mt. Pleasant. Sometimes a family member would drive me directly to Lansing and I would hitchhike up from there. One time I was hitchhiking south with a friend when we were caught in a major snowstorm just south of Brighton near Whitmore Lake on US 23 when the road closed. Up to our knees in snow, we struggled off the road and soon saw, through the blizzard, a small house with a porch light on. It was dark and windy and very cold. A nice couple let us in and I used their phone to call Carol and in about an hour my father-in-law, J.D., came to rescue us in a 4-wheel-drive pickup.

For some unknown reason I was transferred to a brand-new dormitory building on the north edge of campus called Thorpe Hall. My suite was on the fourth floor and shared with three other students. It had its own kitchenette and a bathroom with shower. It was a really nice upgrade.

Tim Dyer had previously made arrangements with Eastern Michigan University that if at the end of my first semester, and my grades qualified, I could transfer to his alma mater for the rest of my college days. I majored in history and geography, with a minor in political science and civics. I worked full-time while attending Eastern as a full-time student for the next four years.

For our first Christmas in 1962, we lived in the back spare room on Park Street. Mom, Jim and Jerry had already decorated a beautiful tree in the living room, but I wanted a Christmas tree to call our own, so I drove to the tree lot located at the Dairy Queen on Wayne Road. I walked around and examined lots of trees but couldn't find any in my price range. The tree man eventually came up to me and asked, "Did you find a tree that you want to buy?" I said, "Well it's the first tree with my wife and, unfortunately, I don't see anything here that we can afford." He said, "Follow me." We went back to the alley where he began sorting through a pile of trees before grabbing one that he set aside, shook the snow off, and asked me if this tree would be OK. Actually, the tree looked crooked and scrawny, with some broken and missing limbs. It stood about 5 feet tall. It wasn't much of a tree. "That's a pretty ugly Christmas tree sir, how much do you want for it?" "2 bits!" So, I gave him a quarter and threw it in the trunk of the car. That's how we got our first "Charlie Brown" Christmas tree. My mother must have laughed for 5 minutes after we stood it up in the corner of our little room. Well … I knew I wanted to get a special tree for our first Christmas together, maybe not like this one, but it's one we never forgot.

In January 1963 I officially began classes at Eastern. We bought our first car, a small green 1955 English Ford that was made in England, from our high school friend Sally Babel's father for $500. It had a stick shift on the floor, and we could barely fit 4 people in it.

*   *   *

March 7, 1963, our beloved daughter Joan Carol Hisey was born in Wayne's Annapolis Hospital. She weighed 7 lbs. 12 oz. and was the prettiest baby in the nursery.

It is difficult to overestimate the dilemma Carol and I found ourselves in. Adulthood was daunting, fatherhood was frightening and scary. Teenagers without any money and a future without means to acquire any. Parenthood to a child while still children ourselves. Of course, we received support from our two families, not in a monetary sense but in countless acts of patience, assistance, and love.

For a short while in the evenings after school, I started delivering pizzas for D'Angelo's Italian Restaurant in Garden City. After Joan was born, we moved into F-8 Pinegrove Terrace, EMU's onsite married student housing. That summer I worked part-time for Lou Singer. He would pick me up in Ypsilanti and we would drive to his new house site just west of Ann Arbor. I helped two or three days a week, starting from the ground up. We staked out the building and helped dig the footings for the basement. I was a mason and carpenter helper from the framing all the way up through the process of installing the shingles and windows. I became good friends with Lou and his wife. He was a smart man and a good mentor as I began to learn the complex mechanics of simple construction. Fate.

Most afternoons I would work at Clark Block and Supply, Carol's family-owned business, running errands and occasionally helping with the block machine as a manual laborer. After hours, my main job was to clean the cement mixer by climbing into the hopper (after carefully checking the fuse box) with a small sledgehammer and a chisel and then just bang away. I still have scars on my hands from my work inside the mixer. When time permitted, I continued to paint.

In the fall of 1963, we bought the 8' x 37' 1953 house trailer from Carol's mom and dad that they had kept at Woodland Lake for $950. It was delivered to lot number 76 at a mobile home park on Harris Rd., just south of Michigan Ave. in Ypsilanti. We lived there until late 1965. I also started to work midnights at Roy's Squeeze Inn, a small hamburger joint on Michigan Ave., just east of the Huron River for $1.25 an hour. My duties included cleaning the grills, washing pots and pans, mopping floors, and scrubbing toilets, and doing the laundry, etc. Usually, I would get done between 6:30 and 7:00 a.m., and depending on my class schedule, would go directly to school to sit by myself, as an outcast, smelling like old grease and garbage.

* * *

Jon's first attempt at carpentry for trailer addition.

Thursday, November 22, 1963, Carol called me from work at the Block plant. It was an early afternoon at the trailer while I was studying for an exam. She said, "President Kennedy has been shot!" A horrific historical multifaceted twist of fate for the Kennedy family and us as a nation and the entire world. There are still reverberations of the third shot of a 6.5 mm caliber brass bullet from a $19.95 mail order World War II Italian-made bolt action rifle. I hung up and immediately turned on the little television that had "rabbit ears" for an antenna and spent the rest of the day in front of it. That afternoon I called Roy at the Squeeze Inn and told him I was going to Kennedy's funeral and would need three or four days off. He fired me. The one and only job I was ever fired from in my life.

Saturday morning, we dropped Joan off at Carol's parents and started our drive to Washington, DC, with Jerry and Mom in her car. We arrived in Washington that evening, found a room in a suburb and drove down to the Capitol building where the slain president laid in state. The lines were over a mile long to get into the Capitol's rotunda and there were rumors that they were going to soon close the line, so we did not see that part of the event. On Monday morning we decided to go to Arlington National Cemetery where throngs of people were already gathering. We positioned ourselves up a slight hill close to the freshly dug gravesite with a good view. We saw the horse-drawn procession, and the same caisson that carried Abraham Lincoln to Washington's train station to begin the slow trip to Springfield, Illinois, 98 years previously. Kennedy's flag-draped coffin slowly approached to the cadence beat of muffled drums, and the steady clip-clop, clip-clop of the horses' hoofs. Family members, heads of state, gathered close with dignitaries, assorted potentates, former presidents Truman and Eisenhower, England's Winston Churchill, Charles De Gaulle of France, and many of the surviving twentieth century world political icons. We watched and heard Cardinal Cushing perform the presidential burial service. We saw Mrs. Kennedy, then the president's brothers, Robert and Ted, light the eternal flame, to the crisp shrill notes of the bugle's taps. As the crowd started to disperse, we lingered at my request, wanting to be there for the actual burial. A while later there were only a smattering of us left as we inched closer to the casket and watched it slowly disappear into its grave.

The assassination of President Kennedy is a date my generation will always remember. It shocked us. Some say that it was the end of the age of innocence. I was grateful to be a part of and close eyewitness to a fateful and major historical event in our nation's history.

*　*　*

During the spring semester of 1964 my dad called and asked

34

what I was going to do tomorrow. I said, "I was going to work for Lou." He then asked if I wanted to hop on a DC-7 cargo plane from Willow Run Airport, Ypsilanti to Love Field in Dallas, Texas, where JFK landed last year on November 22, alive and departed dead. The next morning, I introduced myself to the pilot and copilot and after a few minutes we were airborne. I sat on a crate without a seat belt located just behind and between the pilots and the cargo. Midway into the flight we ran in to some severe weather; rain was leaking through the windows and the plane was being tossed around like a canary in a hurricane. I was hanging on for anything I could find, grasping for my life, afraid the restraints holding the cargo in place would snap under the strain and kill us. We finally got to Dallas and taxied up to the freight hangar. When I got off the airplane, I interrupted the pilots as they started to examine the plane's exterior and said, "I think I'm going to walk back." They laughed while I turned and waved goodbye.

Just outside the airport I stuck my thumb out to hitch a ride and made it all the way to Kansas City that evening. The next day I got a short ride to Independence, Missouri, and toured President Truman's Library. While walking back to the main road I passed the Truman home, hoping I might see the president on one of his frequent walks to his library. Soon I got a ride to St. Louis and rode up to the top of the just completed "Gateway to the West Arch." The next morning, I bought a cheap one-way train ticket on the Lincoln Express to Springfield, Illinois, where I toured the environs of my favorite president, Abraham Lincoln. Afterwards, I took a bus ride to Oak Ridge Cemetery where Lincoln's body was finally permanently laid to rest on September 26, 1901. His remains had been moved seven times since his death in 1865 within the cemetery to thwart any future attempts to steal his remains by body snatchers. His lead-lined coffin was cut open to the light of day for the last time. His face and whiskers had not changed very much but his Brooks Brothers black suit was spotted with some yellow mold and his black bowtie had a red smudge. His casket was manhandled into the just completed new tomb and into a heavy steel frame ten feet below the floor before being buried with solid Portland cement. From there, I hitchhiked to Evanston, Illinois, and spent my last night in a dumpy hotel.

* * *

I think at an early age I grasped the inevitable ending of everyone's story. I knew then that I didn't want my life condensed onto a 5" × 8" index card for an unknown clergyman to read a worn page of his bible that he cannot see to an audience that cannot hear, while thinking of something else. Mortality was my motivator. It was never money or the want of it. The numbers within my story are just numbers that reflect value or worth, from the price of bread to the cost of waterfront property. Numbers are just numbers, not an attempt of aggrandizement or braggadocious. Just a reference between then and now. My time to your time.

During the spring semester of 1964 I became a member of the Army's Reserve Officer Training Corps (ROTC). Rising to the rank of sergeant. And four young men with long hair that called themselves the Beatles invaded America without a shot... seems like "Yesterday."

March 18, 1964, our son and my namesake Jon Clark Hisey was born at Beyer Hospital in Ypsilanti, Michigan, weighing 8 lbs. 10oz. My lifelong helper.

Later that spring I added onto our trailer home with an 8' x 20' lean-to shed. It provided us with a bedroom and small living area. Most of the material was obtained by raiding the construction dumpster at Eastern's new field house building site and picking up used windows and other material from resale stores, including an old pot-bellied wood burning stove that got so hot the first time we used it that the window next to it cracked. I made two bunks for the children in the back bedroom that used to be Carol's and mine, and put tar paper on the new roof, but during winter storms, snow would blow in between the shed roof and the trailer. One of us would turn on our electric blanket, a gift from Grandma Lois, then wait a few minutes for it to warm up before making our wild dash to the bed, quickly getting under the covers, and pulling them up over our heads.

In April, our neighbor across the street was working at Northwest Airlines as a baggage handler at Willow Run Airport. He told me they were hiring in preparation for moving and expanding operations to the newly expanded Detroit Metropolitan Airport in Romulus. A day after I filled out an application at the Willow Run hangar, they put me on a plane to Minneapolis/St. Paul, Minnesota, their home base, for an interview and within a week I was hired with a pay of $368 per month. Only 19 at the time, I was the youngest ticket agent in Detroit, working afternoons and some nights while still carrying a full load of classes at Eastern.

*   *   *

On August 18, 1965, I flew by myself to Anchorage, Alaska, via Portland, Oregon, on Northwest Airlines for a week with $100 cash in my pocket (popularity of bank cards was a few years away). The flight over the Alaskan mountain range was absolutely stunning, but while descending into Anchorage my eardrums would not equalize. The stewardess tried to show me different ways of clearing my ears, but nothing seemed to work, and by the time we landed, I was frantic with pain. A bus delivered me to the Sheraton Hotel (airline discount) in downtown Anchorage where there was a small gift shop in the lobby. I bought a small tin of twelve aspirin before going up to my room, thinking of my impending death. I took 6 aspirin, laid down and woke up the next morning fine. What a relief, spent the entire day walking throughout the city, still visible with the effects of the notorious 9.2 Alaskan earthquake of Good Friday, March 1964. I took a several-hour bus tour to Portage Glacier and a ski chair lift to the top of Alyeska Mountain.

The following morning, I decided to take the train that traveled between Anchorage and Fairbanks, with several small towns and homestead stops along the way and to pick up hunters with their kills and campers with their packs. The train's conductor, Don Prince, befriended me and explained all the stops and scenery that we were going through. He also took me to the engine room where I "helped" drive for a short time. We passed Denali National Park, the base of the highest mountain peak in North America, called Mt. McKinley at the time. In 1975, it was officially changed to its original Indian name "Denali," meaning "The High One." As we were pulling into Fairbanks late that afternoon, Don asked me where I was going to stay, and I said, "Not sure." He walked me across the railroad yard to the old Wayfarer Hotel where some of the rail crew stayed and introduced me to a guy at the front desk. He said, "Our friend here is on a budget and needs a place to stay, so help him out." He turned to leave and said, "I will see you tomorrow, Jon." There were two twin beds crammed into the small room. The bathroom was down the hall and supposedly came with a roommate named Earl that was a dishwasher. There were a few of his personal belongings and a hand towel resting on top of a small, old, light-green painted chest of drawers that I never opened. There was a small photo frame laying down flat. I picked it up and saw a faded black and white photo of a young man and a boy. I laid it back down. I never saw Earl.

I had dinner at the Golden Nugget Saloon and met a nuclear physicist from Purdue, who couldn't believe that I was married with two children and was wandering around Alaska. The return trip to Anchorage was just as spectacular, a wonderful, unforgettable experience. Don Prince was definitely a prince. Fate.

That night back in Anchorage I stayed in a rooming house bunkroom with two or three other guys. One that I remember was an interesting Alaskan bush pilot. In the morning, I left my gear at the front desk and told them I was going to look around and would be back. I walked down to the corner and put my thumb out to see what would happen. Two rides later I found myself traveling with a salesman who was heading to Glennallen, Alaska, on scenic Highway 2, surrounded by glaciers and postcard after postcard of magnificent mountain views.

It was getting late in the day when he said he would drop me off at this little restaurant called the Eureka Lodge about 20 miles ahead which should give me plenty of time to catch a ride back. The Lodge had a few rooms to rent and a small, casual restaurant with some dinette tables covered in worn laminate and a small counter with taped red backless vinyl stools. After a cheeseburger and Coke, I was heading to the bathroom, when in an alcove off the right side of the hallway I saw a huge stuffed brown grizzly bear standing on his hind legs with his arms up and his mouth and eyes wide open looking down at me. Standing up he must have been 8 to 9 feet tall! He was frightening. Before I left the restaurant I asked the waitress, "Wow! that's a big bear, where did it come from?" She said, "The owner shot it five or six years ago behind the restaurant. He thinks it was a state record, but he never had it officially confirmed." I asked with a look of concern written on my face, "Do you have a lot of bears around here?" She replied, "Not too many, but you always have to be on the lookout; this is wild Alaska."

I walked across the two-lane highway and waited for a ride. There was not a lot of traffic. An occasional pickup truck or a big rig would come by, ignoring my extended fist with a thumb sticking out at the end of it. After a while, the sun began to hit the top of the tall mountains to the west and my nerves were moving up to my chest. It seemed like a half hour had passed before anything went by when I finally saw in the distance some sort of vehicle coming. It would disappear into the valley and reappear as a car a few miles away heading toward me. Now I was really getting seriously nervous. The sun's pace quickened, and I could see my shadow in its afterglow of the summer's light night. I was determined not to let this car go by, no matter what. I stood out in the traffic lane and started waving my arms, all the while looking for a bear! As the car approached, I didn't think it was going to stop. But it did. I guess he didn't want to kill me.

The car was an older four-door 1955 Buick sedan. In it was the driver and his wife with an infant in the front seat. I could see the backseat was occupied with an elderly grandmother and two small children. I explained my situation to the man and wife; I had to get back. They said, "We're so sorry but as you can see, we don't have any room for you. We have been on the road for over a week driving back from Indiana." I interrupted, "I'm desperate and scared. I think I can make this work." As the driver released his foot from the brake and the car started to roll, I simultaneously opened the rear door and picked up a child and placed it on my lap and squeezed in next to the grandmother and the other child. I shut the door and locked it, as the car's forward speed increased. They were the nicest people that I could have ever asked for. They delivered me to the front of my rooming house about 10:00 p.m., tired and hungry. Luck.

I have been helped countless times in my travels by the simple acts of kindness from strangers. Albeit sometimes reluctantly. The next day I flew from Anchorage to Seattle and stayed a night at the YMCA. I bought three souvenirs at a little shop next to the bus station for Carol, Joan, and Jon before flying back to Detroit where Carol picked me up with only some small change left in my pocket.

In the fall we traded our expanded trailer home for a camper trailer and a shot gun. We never used either one. We sold them before moving into apartment C107 Cornell Courts, EMU married student housing, and were driving a 1953 Ford that I bought for $150. During 1965 we reported a total income of $3,386.

If you spend money like you don't have any, you will always have some. —JAH

In May of 1966, I bought my first motorcycle, a 50cc Suzuki from a dealer on Washtenaw Ave., just a few miles from school. When taking delivery, the salesman asked if I wanted to get some lessons or if I had any questions about the new motorcycle. I said "No … it's like riding a bike … right?" On my way back to Cornell Courts I encountered my first slight bend in the road, and unable to make a small turn, the bike tipped over and scratched both it and me.

Later that year I flew to Switzerland for a five-day promotional trip sponsored by Northwest Airlines and the InterContinental Hotel in Geneva for $99. I was young and naive. One evening after dinner at a small side-street restaurant, I remember strolling along a boulevard just looking in shop windows as the streetlights powered up. A nice, well-dressed lady approached me from the corner and joined me. After a few paces together she asked, in an attempt to speak English, "Are you lonesome?" I replied, "No. I don't think so." We stopped at the curb, and she waved with an open hand and said, "My place." We stood there looking at each other's faces under a soft light. "Are you uncomfortable?" she asked. "Yes, actually, I wish I had worn my tennis shoes, my feet are killing me." With a delicate wisp of a kiss on my cheek, I got my first strong scent of French perfume before she disappeared into a dark side street, leaving only the sound of her high heeled shoes.

My airline travel benefits allowed me multiple trips, to places such as Nassau, Washington DC, Miami, Chicago, San Juan, and New York City for the 1964–65 World's Fair, where Carol and Mom went with me. In my short career at Northwest Airlines, I was able to accumulate over 100 takeoffs and landings, and to make an educated guess, it would be the beginning of accumulating well over 1500 takeoffs and landings to date. From our early days together, Carol has acquiesced to my natural inclination of wanderlust.

Most of my tenure at Northwest Airlines was spent working afternoons at the ticket counter or the departure gate until the last flight of the day. While on duty at the ticket counter I often needed to and enjoyed making terminal wide "announcements" to call pending flight departure warnings, flight delays, or announcing Mr. so and so to proceed to a departure gate immediately. In those days you had to use the individual's honorifics such as Dr., Mr., Mrs., or Miss, and Master was typically used for a single young man.

One evening my supervisor, Dan Wilson, gave me a folded piece of paper and said, "This young man needs to get back to the ticket counter now. Make a full terminal announcement." He then disappeared behind the office door. I quickly picked up the announcement phone handle, and lowered my voice to my authoritarian tone, "Attention please, attention please, Master Bates, Master Bates, please come to the Northwest Airlines ticket counter. Master Bates, Master Bates, please come quickly to the Northwest Airlines ticket counter." Before I could return the phone to its cradle, I knew something was amiss. My coworkers behind the counter were laughing, my supervisor came out of the office laughing, and a few customers standing in front of the counter joined in the fun.

That winter I applied for a student teaching certificate, and we moved to a rental duplex at 2161 Ackley St. in Wayne for $120 a month and bought our first brand new car, a dark blue stick shift Volkswagen with a manual crank skylight for $1950. Mom had to co-sign the bank loan. In September of 1966, I reluctantly left Northwest Airlines during a labor strike.

Around this time, my dad told me about a small airport in Plymouth, Michigan, that offered to exchange flying lessons for advertising in the *Dispatch* newspapers. After flight class work and over 30 hours of air-time lessons in a 150 Cessna, including several routine touch and go landings and engine stalls and recoveries over Lake Erie, my instructor told me that I had a light touch and was ready for my next step in the process of getting my license. A solo flight, just me without him. I never went back. I really enjoyed my time flying with my instructor sitting beside me. I think I decided then that I knew I couldn't fly but knew that I could swim and successfully spent my life in and around water as much as possible.

* * *

Within a week or two of leaving NWA someone suggested to me that I may find work at Ford Motor Co. I interviewed and was hired as a traffic analyst in their automotive assembly division with a base salary of $284 per week. The office was located near Southfield and Outer Drive, next to Ford's test track and Henry Ford Village in Dearborn. I enjoyed working at Ford, a white collar and tie job in a large room with about 20 men (I was the youngest by several years) and two secretaries, and the boss. My task was to call assembly plants in the USA and Canada each morning and record what the vehicle production was for the last 24 hours. I would then make the necessary calculations on an old 50-pound Freiden adding/calculator machine before calling the different railroad companies to tell them how many bi-level and tri-level railroad cars were needed to haul away the new cars and trucks. One day my boss called me into his office, threw me his car keys, and said "Go to the lot and buy a cheap car for my wife." I didn't know there was a lot, before one of my coworkers told me it was down the road a few miles and contained executive "slightly used" cars they would test drive for a while. I picked out a compact Ford Falcon with a stick shift, about as cheap as you could get. I met some good friends during my short time at Ford. One was a member of the ski patrol at Boyne Highlands and on two weekends I drove up with him and fellow patrollers while staying at some A-frame cabins in Harbor Springs.

* * *

In July 1967, deadly racial riots erupted in downtown Detroit that lasted a few days, and unfortunately, the industrial capital of the Midwest never fully recovered to its glory days as the fifth largest city in our country.

In the spring of 1968 one morning at work, I received an unexpected call from my dad who wanted to have lunch with me. We ate in the executive dining room located within our building. He told me he was thinking of selling *The Wayne Dispatch* newspapers and if he couldn't do that, he was ready to let them die, which he preferred not to do. He went on to explain that he was reluctant to put anymore of his remaining assets into the paper. The business was changing from a hot lead type process to the new cold type method and the competition of the *Wayne Eagle*'s circulation and advertising revenue had grown to over three times that of the *Dispatch*. He was now focused on another flying freight business that he had started with a partner. As a child, I was accustomed to "hanging around" the newspaper office and printing plant on Main Street, only a few blocks from my

home. It had a large old-fashioned rotary press and noisy lino-
type machines where deaf and nonverbal people sat with the hot
lead that formed the type for the presses. It was all empty now.
Dad had lost his fight with the union and during Wayne's disastrous urban renewal plan, the city bought the paper's building and
tore it down. It was a ghost of itself; only six or seven employees
were left to produce some papers with fancy electronic typewrit-
ers, and an advertising salesman who doubled as a manager. They
operated out of a city worn-out, vacant storefront building. The
papers were printed by a company called Inco Graphics in a suburb of Lansing.

Carol and I talked about the proposition for a few days, before
hesitantly agreeing to take over the paper. It was a very casual
arrangement, no contract, no paperwork. When my name first
appeared in the *Dispatch*, I became the youngest managing edi-
tor/newspaper publisher as a member of the Michigan Press
Association, the captain of a sinking ship. What was I thinking?
We had zero idea of what we were doing, or even how to do it if
we did.

When I left Ford, my coworkers gave me a retirement party at
a nice upscale restaurant in downtown Dearborn. They gave me
a few gifts and a card signed by all my Ford friends and bosses
including Henry Ford II … (it surprised me too). The only retirement party I ever had — age 23.

*   *   *

After a short few months my paychecks from the *Dispatch* started
to bounce. Dad told us he could no longer afford to put any more
money into the paper. He had hoped the transition could have
been longer but his new freight venture (that dissolved within a
year or two) was taking more money than he had planned, and
this was the way it had to be. He was done. Dad had made his

choice, and unfortunately, we had no choice. We were set adrift, left to our own resourcefulness. Hmmm, sounds familiar.

From that day forward, and for the rest of our lives, our only income, every nickel, every quarter, every dollar, was generated by initiative, ingenuity, hard work, fate and luck, lots of luck.

In 1968, we purchased our first home at 3318 Hubbard St. in Wayne, just north of Michigan Avenue, for $24,500 in a very desirable upscale neighborhood. Ours was the first house on the street next to a gas station (not too upscale). It had three bed-rooms, 1½ bathrooms, and an in-ground concrete Esther Williams swimming pool. The following year I built an eight-foot-tall jump platform with four posts buried into the ground with a piece of plywood on top. It had no guardrails and only a small target area of deep water in the pool that you had to aim for. When an adult did a cannonball, it seemed the pool would lose about an inch of water. The next summer we installed a commercial size in-ground trampoline. It's a miracle we all survived unhurt. Our backyard became famous for large Fourth of July family and guest parties.

A little over a year after taking control of the newspaper, I started negotiating with Roger Turner, the award-winning man-aging editor of the *Wayne Eagle* newspaper. The *Eagle* was an upstart newspaper about 15–20 years old and had surpassed our paper in circulation and advertising revenue by a wide margin. They were a fierce competitor and Roger had the support of sev-eral qualified staff reporters. After a few all-night sessions at our home with Roger, his Pall Mall cigarettes, and his never-ending coffee with two creams and two sugars, I convinced him to join me by giving him full control of all editorial content as managing editor. I would remain publisher.

Again, no contract or paperwork except maybe some notes on a paper napkin somewhere that I don't recall ever seeing. I had already decided to change the size of the paper from a broadsheet to a tabloid, along with a new masthead logo and format. Shortly after Roger was hired, he introduced me to George Moses, a top-notch advertising salesman from the Brighton, Michigan, area. He came onboard to sell and oversee all advertising.

Also, about this time, I started a stand-alone new company called Metro Graphics which contracted graphic design and key lining for all the *Dispatch* publications and other newspapers, as

The Wayne Dispatch

well as in-house newsletters and other printing needs. It was created to oversee and coordinate all operations of the newspaper. Roger and I often argued over the business side and the cost of the editorial side, but we remained awkward friends to the end. He taught me how to play golf.

One employee we hired as a high school reporter stands out. His name was Phil Cousineau. He eventually became a student mentored by Joseph Campbell in California, a well-known American writer of mythology and comparative religion. Campbell was a philosopher who hosted a popular television series on PBS called *The Power of Myth*. Phil became a well-known author of more than 30 books, a poet, philosopher, public speaker, travel guide, and TV personality who often acknowledges his first job as a cub reporter for *The Wayne Dispatch*.

*   *   *

1968–69 was a tumultuous time in American history. Civil rights leader Martin Luther King Jr. was assassinated in Memphis, Tennessee in April and presidential primary candidate Senator Robert F. Kennedy was killed by an assassin's bullet in a kitchen hallway of the Ambassador Hotel in Los Angeles, California, in June. Opposition to the Vietnam War and the much-needed Civil Rights movement was boiling over. This period would eventually be considered a defining point in our history.

That winter the city moved the *Dispatch* and graphics business into another urban renewal building, the old Young Hardware, where just a few years prior my friend and I had purchased a new lawnmower, located at the corner of Park St. and South Wayne Rd. It was a much better and bigger location. In the front corner there was a small unused area of about 400 square feet. A friend of mine, Emil Gervais, that I had met in the Wayne Jaycee's Service Club, approached me with an idea to start an office supply business in that little corner. Emil was a salesman for a major auto supply warehouse company. He and I were to be 50/50 partners. The evening before we were scheduled to file our partnership papers and open a bank account with $500 each, he and his wife invited us to their house. After some small talk, they informed us that the office supply business was too much of a risk for them and they were sorry, but they changed their minds, even though Emil was going to keep his day job.

Avoiding failure is the same as failing. —JAH

In March of 1969 Carol and I opened Suburban Office Supplies with $500, the total of all our bank savings accounts. We had no experience in any retail business and even less in the products we were attempting to sell. I found an office products wholesaler, located near the river in Detroit's old warehouse district. The salesman came to our corner location in Wayne. After I told him we wanted to start our business with a $500 order, he had to apologize for his constrained laughter. He made a start-up order from his own experience and told me it was too small for his company to deliver. He said, "You can pick it up tomorrow afternoon and bring a check." The next afternoon my five-year-old son Jon and I loaded up our station wagon and wrote our first check from our new office supply account for $509.20. Nine dollars and twenty cents overdrawn. As soon as we got back to the shop, I told Carol about the overdraft. She immediately left without a word and from somewhere in the house, she never told me where, she found twenty dollars to deposit into our new bank account near closing time. *What a way to start a business!* You won't find that in any business textbook. We learned as we went along. All product inventory, all systems, all protocol, all forms, and order systems were created from scratch.

A few days after we opened the office supply business, we

closed it for two weeks while Carol and I took our first trip west to ski in Vail, Colorado, where I traded advertising for a week at Rams Horn Lodge. I had priorities that mattered. We had leased a new four-door Thunderbird from Jack Demmer Ford by also trading lease expenses for newspaper advertising. Jack was a World War II airplane pilot, a good guy. I became quite an expert at living large with small earnings.

While driving up Vail Pass at night in an ever-worsening snowstorm, the car stopped forward progress in the ice and snow and began slipping and sliding, moving backward down the hill. I had little control. After regaining some traction, we managed to find a parking spot at a small restaurant lodge that we had noticed earlier. I went in to see about a room for the night, expecting to sleep on the dining room floor, while Carol stayed in the car praying for a room and our safety. Luckily, we got the last room. In the morning, we bought tire chains from a gas station next door and finished our drive over Vail Pass and into the ski resort. We were wonderstruck by the majestic beauty of the Rocky Mountains and fell in love with the slopes and the new small town of Vail.

In the summer of 1969, Wayne celebrated its one-hundred-year anniversary. As a centennial committee member, I was put in charge of designing and printing the booklet of events and history of the city. In front of the library on the corner of Sims St. and Wayne Road, we buried a time capsule next to a freshly planted oak tree. At the last moment before the lid was set, I threw in my credit cards, driver's license, photos of my children, and some money. It is to be opened in 2069. I hope someone will be there to open it and claim your inheritance.

* * *

In July 1969, Dad and I were able to obtain three press passes for NASA's *Apollo 11* moon launch. I drove south to Cape Canaveral, which had recently changed its name to Cape Kennedy, with

Dad and Darleen. On the 15th of July in the early afternoon, we picked up brother Jim from Connecticut, at the Orlando Airport and then drove to the Space Center on Florida's east coast. Darleen dropped the three of us off at the press entrance to pick up our credentials and information packet and then traveled by a NASA bus with several other reporters to the Public Relations building that was located close to the oversized digital countdown clock that has become an iconic space launch symbol. We casually spent the rest of the day touring the grounds, outbuildings, and VIP section while waiting for our press briefings in the auditorium. An air of excitement enveloped the environment. Top level national and international newspaper reporters and TV news personalities mingled among us. I can remember seeing Walter Cronkite of CBS, Jay Barbree and Frank McGee of NBC, and Frank Reynolds from ABC.

We were grateful for the complimentary sandwiches, snacks, coffee, and sodas that were provided all day and evening. Eventually, after sunset, the three of us went our separate ways to find a place to nap, read, or eat.

Early in the morning, around 4:00 a.m., I heard an announcement that a bus was leaving for the astronaut training building at about 5:00. Astronauts Armstrong, Aldrin, and Collins were dressed and preparing to have the traditional steak and egg breakfast. I grabbed one of the last seats. The bus drove us out to launch pad 39 A and slowly circled the magnificent Saturn 5 rocket, just waiting for its chance at history. It was enormous, shining bright white next to the red/orange gantry under the glow of massive lights. It looked like it was breathing as it vented steam from bleeder valves of pressurized liquid fuel mixed with Florida's warm air. It was huge. This three-stage rocket, taller than the Empire State Building, was beautiful, slender, and awe-inspiring with a small capsule point at its top that would soon be home to three men. Standing tall, balanced momentarily secured to Earth by four massive clamps, proud, pointing to space, a bright light against a still quiet dark night.

On the way back to the Press Center we stopped at the astronaut operations building and got off the bus. In a few minutes word came that the three experienced intrepid space travelers were about to come out and get into their waiting Astro van that would deliver them to the rocket. Unbelievable, me standing there, one of over 3.5 billion people in the world, front row, maybe 20 or 30 feet away as I waved to the three men dressed in space suits carrying air conditioner packs on their way to history. And they waved back. Was it a wave of hi, or a wave of goodbye?

I was among the fortunate because it was the only bus of the pre-launch morning spectacle. Luck.

After the bus ride to launch pad 39 A and the operations building, there were still a few hours left on the large countdown clock. I tried to nap, without success, in the briefing auditorium between frequent intercom announcements and news talking reporters. After more coffee and pastries, I met Dad and Jim among the growing crowd of news people. The newcomers were fresh looking with expensive cameras and new unopened reporter notepads. Together, the three of us drifted to the adjacent VIP bleacher section located next to the press area where Vice President Spiro Agnew, past President Lyndon Johnson and his wife, Ladybird, and an assortment of celebrities were settling in. The most memorable to me was the sight of Charles Lindbergh, who only 42 years earlier (May 1927) piloted the single-engine, fuel-laden *Spirit of St. Louis* airplane nonstop across the Atlantic Ocean from New York's Roosevelt's grass runway to the city of Paris, France, in 34 hours, landing amongst a crowd of thousands at Le Bourget airfield. Hard to imagine that there were only twenty years between Lindbergh and Yeager and only another fourteen years from Yeager to Alan Shepard.

NASA's announcements routinely gave us status reports of

the crew, their capsule, the launch pad, and mission control. You could sense the rise of excitement. After a few small countdown pauses, the big clock pegged the ten-minute mark and the talk turned to the realization that we were about to witness one of the, if not the, greatest engineering achievements in all of human history.

The press area was less than three miles from the rocket. A little closer than the VIP section and theoretically the closest safe distance from a calamity of a colossal simultaneous explosion of over six million pounds of high-tech rocket fuel. The tidewaters of Banana River casually meander through the Cape and help define the "safe zone" barrier. Only a few NASA emergency personnel were located in a windowless bunker buried deep near the rocket were closer. By the T minus five-minute mark, I had successfully maneuvered myself next to the shore of the enlarged segment of the river that was closest to the launch pad. I was standing between national reporters of consequence and NASA photographers with expensive two- and three-foot long lenses affixed on tripods and with strings of important credentials draped around their necks.

T minus 30 seconds, the loudspeakers declared. I briefly glanced to my left and right, then eased my way down to the grassy bank of the river's marshland. My shoes made an imprint in the wet sand, being sure to stake my claim of being the closest. Unlike astronauts' footprints on the moon that will last for eons, mine will be gone with the afternoon tide, but the imprint in my mind will never disappear. At 9:32 a.m. EST, T minus 10 seconds, the crowd's countdown became louder each second by the thousands of witnesses giving testimony to a monumental modern miracle. I didn't blink; I didn't hold my hands over my ears or use the NASA earplugs. I stood there at attention with my chest out and chin up, embracing the moment, joining the chorus in unison, 5 ... 4 ... 3 ... You see the explosion first. The rockets telegraphed their might through the earth into my shoes and into my spine and into my soul. It was the loudest noise made by man ever recorded. It invades every nerve cell in your body, every atom, every molecule, senses of sound, touch, fear, and excitement all coalesced together. The rocket moved, just a little, straining with all its power of the controlled explosion. It slowly crawled its way up next to the gantry, defying gravity, defying logic, defying Newton, defying history, defying God almighty. We all started to say Go! The go's got louder with each second, the rocket got faster, soon everyone was yelling together GO … GO … GO Baby GO … GO. Come on Baby GO! Tears of emotion clouded my eyes. The sound of our yells replaced the fading roar of the rocket as it burned its way through over 4 1/2 million pounds of fuel and reaching a speed of over 6,000 miles an hour in just its first two minutes. The rocket's roar evaporated into the morning sky, and we gawked as it disappeared from the bright light of Florida's summer sky to the deadly cold of black space as it vanished, leaving only a scribbled contrail in its wake. Off they went. Three courageous mortal souls, to an immortal destiny.

I was there, front of the front. Thank you. Thank you. Thank you, I was a witness. Extraordinary luck and fate.

I never forgot those moments; how could I ever forget? I can only hope my last thought of silent consciousness, after my family goodbyes, as I start my final journey will be of "Go … Go Baby Go … Go Baby Go," on my way back to the Stars.

THE SEVENTIES

EXCITING DAYS OF GROWTH

THE DECADE OF THE '70S was an amazing time of growth and detailed dedication from Carol and me to Parkway Office Supply and our precious growing family.

The years also brought an end to NASA's $25 billion Apollo moon program when in December 1972 Commander Gene Cernan shut the door of the lunar module. After 75 hours, he and Harrison Schmitt explored the moon with the help of a four-wheel drive lunar roving vehicle and said, "America's challenge today has forged man's destiny of tomorrow … and God willing, we shall return, with peace and hope for all mankind." That tomorrow is still tomorrow.

Our country's population was just over 205 million. Unprecedented tumultuous political drama continued to fester, and the Vietnam War finally ended unceremoniously with over 58,000 US fatalities. In the summer of 1974, Nixon's Watergate scandal eventually caused him to be the first president to resign, after leadership of his own Republican party told him that they were going to impeach him. It was the honorable choice that resulted in Michigan's Congressman Gerald Ford becoming our country's first unelected president.

The notorious Woodstock, New York, landmark music festival

joined the developing revolt and sex and drugs were starting their social revolution. Music has always been my drug of choice, and it was first delivered by an innocent needle at the end of my record player's tonearm. Two computers were connected at the University of California, which some came to view as the start of the internet, and Apple Computer was founded shortly thereafter in April 1976 by two college dropouts. Eventually forever changing the world in both good and bad ways. Global warming and climate change warnings were first being discussed by scientists and, unfortunately, challenged and disregarded by political leaders and corporate greed.

"Isn't it a pity . . . isn't it a shame." —G.H.

Fashion became "unusual." Men wore bell-bottom pants, colorful jackets, and shoulder-length hair (not me). Women wore leisure suits, jumpsuits, and very short miniskirts (not me).

*   *   *

When we tried to incorporate Suburban Office Supply with the state of Michigan, we were informed that the name was already being used in Rochester, Michigan, so we changed the name to Park (street I grew up on) way (first three letters of Wayne) "Parkway Office Supply, Inc." In March the office supply business was growing so fast that we bought a new Ford Econoline delivery van.

In December 1970, we purchased our first commercial building at 3158 S. Wayne Rd., on the corner of Elm for $30,000 on a land contract of $25,000 ($5,000 down) from Mark and Bertha Eudaly. After a few modifications we moved the *Wayne Dispatch,* Metro Graphics and our new office supply business, which was consuming much more of my attention. We split the building in two, about 1,000 sq. ft for the office supply, and 1,800 square feet for *The Wayne Dispatch, Metro Graphics,* and the publishing business.

* * *

On June 5, 1972, our beloved Jenifer Ann was born into our family at 9 lbs. 6½ oz. at Annapolis Hospital and we brought her home in our new Plymouth station wagon.

In the late summer, the five of us drove to northwest Michigan to search for lake property where we could build a cottage. We narrowed our choice between a small lot on Little Traverse Bay of Lake Michigan between Charlevoix and Petoskey, and a nice waterfront piece on Otsego Lake near Gaylord. The four of us (although Jenifer displayed a strong sense of opinion at an early age) decided Jenifer was too young to vote. While driving south we kept going back and forth, undecided which one we liked the best. Finally, about halfway home, we agreed to flip a coin to make the final decision for us. Heads Otsego Lake, tails Lake Michigan. Carol flipped a quarter, slapped it on the back of her hand and with excitement revealed the shiny head of George Washington. OOOH! We all sighed together. After a few minutes of silence, I said, "Let's flip it again!" "Yes!" came the unanimous reply. That's how we ended up in Charlevoix the Beautiful on Lot 37 in Michigan Shores for $9,750.

It was about this time that the friction of the office supply business and the newspaper business came to a point where I realized the burden of the newspaper would never justify my continued involvement. It actually never generated a profit and had accumulated a sizeable debt of about $13,000 to Inco Graphics, our printer in Mason, Michigan. Roger and I reached an agreement for the sale of the business that included Metro Graphics, with generous terms to his benefit. I was relieved from the debt and in addition received a promissory note of $14,000. I was comforted that Roger, and his partners would be able to carry on the legacy of *The Wayne Dispatch*. They moved to a rented warehouse behind Gates Furniture on Michigan Avenue, and we expanded the office supply store. Sadly, within a year (without a payment on their note), they experienced a devastating fire that forced them out of business and the Hisey's family ties to *The Wayne Dispatch* folded into an important part of Wayne's history. A very sad day.

My next motorcycle was a Honda 500cc that I bought from a priest who lived and tended to his flock at the Eloise County Hospital complex. Brother Jerry had a stretched Triumph bike and together we rode our motorcycles north to Charlevoix. We camped on a raised wooden shelf we made between four standing trees at the cottage lot. I remember one morning we biked into town to get some breakfast and supplies. We purchased about a pound of loose nails and put them in a small paper bag that I fastened onto the back seat strap behind me. When we arrived at the lot there were only a few nails left in the bag, I can't imagine how many flat tires I may have caused between Charlevoix and Michigan Shores. Sorry.

* * *

Jessica Louise was born at 9 lb. 6 oz. on May 18, 1974, on my 30th birthday to complete our family. I can't imagine a more precious gift a father could have.

In the summer we rented an A-frame style house on McSauba Rd. in Charlevoix and started to build our cottage on Little Traverse Bay. It was a Wicks Home package from Petoskey that cost approximately $6,000. It included all framing material from the block basement up: siding, windows, and shingles. We paid cash, mostly earned by me working alone at Parkway on

Saturdays (two for the store, one for the cottage). After the basement was excavated, I hired a contractor for the footings, lay up the cement block, and pour the concrete floor. From there, with the help of my time with Lou Singer and many family members including Dad, Jerry, and son Jon, we built the whole house by learning as we went along.

Soon after Jessica was born, we purchased 41900 North Drive, our next home, in Canton, Michigan, from Carol's parents, J.D. and Marian Clark. It was first offered to Carol's sister Barb and brother Joel before we accepted, and later that year we sold our home on Hubbard St. to my brother Jerry and Nancy Hisey. That December we spent our first Christmas at our new "Lake House" cottage that was not quite finished but livable and memorable.

Within five years after we started the office supply business it generated gross sales of over $400,000. I came to appreciate early the importance of details. From the grand scheme to the mundane minutiae, details are important. People used to tell me, "Don't sweat the small stuff." I say, "If you sweat the small stuff, you will avoid sweating the big stuff."

We bought a used Sunfish sailboat called *The Pill* from a pharmacist in Harbor Springs. I learned how to sail in Little Traverse Bay in front of the Lake House by the trial and error, wet and wild method that included many tip overs and mouthfuls of lake water. It took most of the summer before Carol and the children would sail with me. It was a wonderful five summers at the Lake House. I would usually commute on weekends by either driving my new used MGB red convertible roadster or by commercial air from Traverse City or Pellston to Detroit.

* * *

Jon, Jessica, and Jenifer on *The Pill*.

In 1976, we bought lot #61 in Michigan Shores. It was off the water, and we built another Wicks Home package that became our first "spec house." For temporary electric service, we ran 250 ft of romax wire from the Lake House, which was later used in the new house. I hired two high school boys from Charlevoix to help with its construction. Son Jon was always there to lend a hand.

In August Carol said she could use a new toaster for her 32nd birthday. Instead, I bought her a new 26' Columbia "shoal keel" sailboat, which we named *Paper Clipper*. We kept it at Maynard's Marina near Gibraltar on the winding Huron River almost a mile inland before emptying into the north end of Lake Erie where it converged with the Detroit River. I became friends with the boat seller and worked two or three boat shows with him as a salesman in Detroit's Cobo Hall and in the Mt. Clemens show on Lake St. Clair.

A sailing day on *Paper Clipper.*

In 1977, we paid off Lot 37 in Michigan Shores and in August bought lots 286 and 287 S. Wayne Rd., Westland from Bill and Faith Gilroy for $20,000 with a $5,400 down payment and a land contract. In November we bought Lots 14, 284, and 285 from the Gilroy's for $29,500 with $4,000 down payment and another land contract. These collective parcels would soon become the new home of a 4,500-square-foot Parkway Office Supply store. We eventually attached four commercial rental units on its north side.

We also started Huron Valley Office Supply, Inc. on Washtenaw Ave., Ann Arbor, Michigan, a few miles west of Eastern Michigan University. We shared the space and expenses with Steve Savoie and Norman MacArther as they started their own business called University Office Equipment. In a few years I sold the office supply business and inventory. Steve and Norm expanded their business to the entire store.

* * *

One summer I started a sailing trip with Dad, Jerry, and Jon on the *Paper Clipper* from Maynard's Marina to Charlevoix/Harbor Springs. During the sail north we encountered calm weather for the first four days before finally sailing into Harrisville, Michigan, our first port of call. The next morning, we had a nice offshore breeze and were excited to finally be sailing at a quick pace. By midday the breeze had strengthened quite a bit, and with the winds steadily increasing, it unfortunately also brought the waves of Lake Huron to a height of 6 to 8+ feet. We were offshore in the middle of Thunder Bay and sailing fast with just a double reefed mainsail when talk started about turning around to the safety of Alpena. We thought we would be safe in the lee of the land once we crossed the open bay. After passing the lighthouse and Coast Guard station at the tip of the bay, there was no lee, there were just more gale force winds and more threatening waves. We decided it was too dangerous to proceed, but first we had to maneuver a tricky 180-degree turn to head back toward Alpena. As we climbed to the top of a big wave, I hollered to be heard above the wind and lake spray, "Come about!" and shoved the tiller hard to starboard into the wind. Unfortunately, at the crest of the wave, the stern of the boat came out of the water as we tried to make the turn. It slammed hard on the way down the backside of the high wave and tore the rudder from the hardware that attached it to the transom of the boat. I put a death grip on the tiller to prevent it from sinking to the bottom of the lake as Jerry and Dad rushed to help pull the heavy rudder up and into the middle of the cockpit.

Now we were rudderless and in the throes of a Lake Huron storm with tall worrisome threatening seas all around. We lowered the 15-hp long-shaft engine (the first time of the trip) and to everyone's relief it started, providing some form of steerage. I then grabbed the marine radio microphone and calmly hailed, "Thunder Bay Coast Guard, Thunder Bay Coast Guard, this is Paper Clipper calling, Thunder Bay Coast Guard, this is sailing vessel Paper Clipper." They answered quickly and I explained the situation and our position, that we were seeking help. They responded. "Yes we see you Paper Clipper, we had our eyes on you as you went by. What are you doing out there in this weather?" I ignored the question. They continued, "Unfortunately, we do not have a boat here capable of coming out in these conditions to help you."

He asked if we were taking on water. I said, "There is a hole in the hull at the water line where the rudder was, but our manual bilge pump is keeping up so far and I do not think we are in danger of sinking." He replied, "We will continue to monitor you, and suggest that you take down your reefed mainsail, and head back under power into Thunder Bay. When you get close to us you will see a small inlet at the base of the station that you will be able to turn into. Some men will be there to guide you and help you dock." We finally arrived about 5:00 p.m., safe and relieved. The crew of the Coast Guard was very accommodating, with good food and clean beds to spend the night in their dorm room where the walls were decorated with magazine pictures of girls that they wished were their wives. They gave young Jon an extra helping of fresh-baked cookies and took him to the top of the lighthouse. I called Carol in Canton from the station and explained the predicament. Then I called Mike, the boat salesman, and luckily, he happened to have a sister ship to *Paper Clipper*. He would remove that tiller and rudder with hardware and set it aside for Carol. The next day Carol and the children picked up the replacement parts and drove to Alpena.

We left the Coast Guard Station the following morning in calm waters and motored the few miles to the Alpena City Marina where a local boatyard mechanic made the necessary repairs shortly after Carol's delivery. We spent the night together before sailing north to Roger City in kind seas. We arrived at Mackinaw City on July 3 where Carol, Mom, Joan, and Jerry's family greeted us, and spent the following two days sailing between the city and Mackinac Island. On July 6 I set sail with timidity from Mackinaw City in an overcast sky with a thin layer of strata clouds with just Joan and Jon for our final destination, Irish Boat Shop in Harbor Springs.

It was a noneventful voyage except when after passing the Waugoshance Point Abandoned Lighthouse and turning 90 degrees to head south, I accidentally jibed the mainsail. It was as loud and as startling as a close buccaneer cannon, surprising all of us. I was standing at the tiller when the boom slammed hard to the starboard railing, just missing me on the side of the head and probably would have knocked me overboard, which would likely have made these memories a little shorter.

In March of 1978, we borrowed $98,000 from Detroit Bank and

Trust and began to construct our new office supply store. I hired Grant Campbell, a local contractor who was recommended by Carol's father. We got along great and worked together on how to solve problems, make changes and save money during construction. I enjoyed the process and became adept at the basics of commercial construction. Family members and I provided some sweat equity before opening on schedule and under budget, which is easy to do if you guess long, and figure high.

* * *

Sometime in the summer Carol started looking in and around Charlevoix for a west-facing piece of property on Lake Michigan to enhance our view of the spectacular techno color sunsets. Eventually, she found a small lot in Charlevoix, a block off the channel at the west end of Pine River Lane. Once I walked the property, I fell in love with it. It was listed for $110,000 and owned by Dr. and Mrs. Saltonstall, a prominent local family. The real estate listing agent was George Richardson. He suggested the idea to build a six-unit condominium and to keep one for ourselves. My first question to George was, *"What the hell is a condominium?"* That is what started my career as a condominium real estate developer in northwest Michigan.

We made an appointment to meet with architect Hans Weimer in his upstairs office in the See Building in downtown Charlevoix. I explained the six-unit condominium plan to Mr. Weimer and how we intended to sell them and to keep one for our family. I finally asked him, "Well … what do you think?" He then proceeded with his slight German accent, to list several issues of uncertainty and potential problems. The one I remembered clearly was the rumored possibility of an Indian burial ground on the property. He summed up the visit with advice not to do it. Discouraged, wearing frowns, we left.

As we walked to our car, I recalled a small, hanging architect's sign pointing to an upstairs office on Bridge Street next to the bridge. We decided to just drop in unannounced to check it out. At the top of the steep, narrow stairs the door was opened into an empty reception/secretary area. We saw a man hunched over a drawing desk, in the next room, listening to classical music. I walked to the arch into his domain and knocked.

No response. I turned to Carol and shoulder shrugged, she whispered, "louder." The man turned with a big welcoming smile with a gap between his front teeth, "Hi, come on in. I'm Jack Begrow." After a few minutes of introductions and small talk and repeating of what I had just told Mr. Weimer, along with a disclosure of ignorance and helplessness, we paused and nervously waited for Jack's reaction. Jack was excited! He knew the property; he thought it was a great idea. He offered to do a quick study of possible configurations, square footages, and current cost analysis projections. He advised us that we would need some preliminary plans and what we could expect a lender might need.

Wow … what a difference that chance meeting made. Sixty minutes, maybe not even an hour. Fate and luck.

This was the start of over a 25-year business relationship and a very good friendship. My next step in becoming a small-town real estate developer was finding a bank to lend an unknown, young 34-year-old pencil salesman from downstate to build a $500,000-plus condominium project in the middle of Charlevoix. Within a week I had presented my plans and projections along with a letter of introduction and short biography of myself to the two local banks in Charlevoix, and one in Petoskey that resulted in rejection and dejection. After telling Jack of the roadblock, he told me of a developer from Shanty Creek in Bellaire that was able to get a construction loan from a bank called Northwestern Savings and Loan in Traverse City. He had no contact name or phone number. Carol, Jenifer, and Jessica drove with me south to Traverse City.

We found the bank at a busy corner in downtown, where I was politely advised that they did not accept business loan applications, but that their new main office on the corner of Garfield and Airport Rd. might. Shortly we found the modern looking bank building, with its hard marble floors like a mausoleum, imposing and very intimidating. I was feeling out of place when I asked a teller who I might speak to for a condominium construction loan. I stood there watching her ask a few dressed-up, important looking men lingering outside their little offices whispering important secrets with faint echoes. She said, "No one here at the moment can help you." I can remember starting to turn when she said, "Oh just a minute, I see Mr. Michael opened his door. Wait here and I will see if he can help you."

It turned out that Mr. Leon Michael was the president of the bank and that he was one of the most gracious and kindest man I had ever met. Carol and the girls were parked right outside his full-length office windows and watched the entire time as I discussed my ideas and showed him our preliminary plans. He asked me several questions about myself and my plans and after some delightful conversation said, "Tell you what Jon, write me a letter reciting what you just told me along with the copies of what Begrow has provided, and I will see what we can do." That began an over 20-year banking business relationship of borrowing well over three million dollars in construction loans. We were fortunate to have never missed a payment and never asked to make adjustments or changes to what was verbally agreed to with a handshake, or a simple phone call.

Mr. Michael was near the top of the list of people who helped me, who saw something in me. I was grateful that he appeared in my life at the right time. In remembering this from the viewpoint of a sentimental old man, maybe he was a father figure to me. Maybe, another Grandpa Simpson. Fate. Maybe. Luck? I don't know.

* * *

I had learned to ski at a young age with a pair of used wood skis with "bear claw bindings." As equipment and my ability progressed, I used metal skis with toe/heel bindings with long leather safety straps. By my 30s, I had become quite a proficient skier when I decided to buy my first fiberglass skis with new modern step-in bindings. Fiberglass changed the sport dramatically. So it was that I found myself at the top of Boyne Highlands in Harbor Springs dressed in my shiny new dark blue ski parka and pants with my new skis, bindings, boots, and poles, ready to make my first trial run down the intermediate Heather slope. It provided a nice incline at the top, and I was full of confidence and ready to start with a nice easy traverse. Going a little faster than I wanted, I unweighted and dropped my shoulder to make my first turn downhill. Nothing happened. Now, going too fast and out of control I found myself heading toward a beginner ski school group lined up attentively listening to their instructor. I decided to make a quick emergency fall to stop, but as I skidded by the last person in line my right ski clipped the front shovel of the beginner's ski. Down she went, falling onto the next skier in line like dominoes; I sat there helpless and watched like a movie in slow motion as everybody was trying to move away from the student next to them. All was in vain until the instructor fell over to end the carnage, all the while screaming at me as he struggled to untangle himself while trying to stand up. "Get out of here! I am going to pull your ticket if I see you again! Get out of my sight! Learn how to ski on the bunny hill before skiing here! Get out of here!"

As I profusely began to apologize, I fumbled my way up to a standing position and started my timid escape, slowly snowplowing straight downhill as my new parka's price tag was flapping in the wind behind me. By the end of the day my new fiberglass skis worked great … and made it much easier to execute parallel turns with grace and style.

In the spring of 1979, we broke ground on the six-unit condominium project that I named "Lake House" on the shores of Lake Michigan and in October we sold the original Lake House cottage for $50,000.

First Lake House, revisited in 2010.

THE EIGHTIES

GLORY DAYS

AT THE START OF THE 1980S A GALLON OF GAS was a little over $1.50, a gallon of milk was only 85 cents, and you could buy a six-pack of beer for $3.50 and watch the University of Michigan beat Michigan State 27 to 23. The personal computer was about to be born and greed was thought to be good and big hair was in. The rise of modern conservatism began with President Reagan's inauguration in January of '81 and the AIDS epidemic terrorized the world with over 40 million deaths worldwide. NASA's space shuttle program began from Cape Kennedy's launch pad 39 on April 12. Ted Turner created CNN, becoming the first 24-hour cable news network in the world. Airline fares became a bargain after the government's deregulation, and passengers were still "dressing up" for the ride, and people only wore tennis shoes to play tennis.

* * *

In January, Bill Meyers, our condominium attorney from Dykema Gossett, which helped write Michigan's condominium laws, a prestigious Southfield law office (think expensive), called me to ask a few questions before he could start the documents for the Lake House. "What is the official name of your development company?" "I don't officially have a development company," I told him. After a few moments, we agreed on J.A.H. Development, Inc. He said, "OK that was easy, what is your Michigan builder's license number?" I said, "I didn't have a builder's license." He said, "I thought you were a builder?" I said, "Kind of." He went on to explain that in Michigan, in order to build and sell condominiums, you are required to have a builder's license, and so does your new corporation.

First condominium project, "The Lake House."

Bill called back in a few days telling me that there was a builders' class that would meet in the evenings in Livonia. They had already started the current class a few weeks ago, but he had made arrangements with the school that allowed me to attend the balance of the term. Five or six weeks later I drove to Lansing to take the builder's license exam. I spent the night in a really cheap motel in a terrible, rundown part of town near the test site. I was nervous about the next day's test, but I was really nervous and scared about where I was spending the night. So, after closing my door for the evening, I jammed a chair between the door lock and the floor and then manhandled the dresser up against the front of the wedged chair. Feeling a little safer, I finally fell asleep. In the morning, I got up at 5:00 a.m. to get ready for the 7:00 a.m. exam. I manhandled the dresser back to where it was, then unwedged the chair that was under the doorknob, set that aside, got my gear together and opened the door to leave and saw to my alarm that I had left the key in the door all night! I passed the test and became a licensed builder in the State of Michigan and kept it until 2008.

On May 18, 1980, my 36th birthday, Carol and the children were in Canton, while I was in Charlevoix to attend my first Lake House closing (one of over an eventual 175 real estate transactions in my career) with customers Bob and Skip Ogle, a Buick dealer from Indianapolis. I went to dinner with Jack and Barb Begrow to celebrate the dual events and spent the night alone on the just carpeted floor of our family's new top floor unit #6 at the Lake House. Mount St. Helens in Washington state violently erupted that day, two consequential coincidental events that are seared into my memory.

Later that year I started Office World, Inc., on Warren Rd. in Dearborn Heights, Michigan, with friend Bob Miles. A 50/50 partnership. Office World lasted only a few years and closed when Bob left to pursue bigger and better opportunities.

* * *

In the spring of 1981, Bob Miles asked me to join him and two of his friends on a trip to the British Virgin Islands. He planned to rent a sailboat, I was the only one with sailing experience, to cruise and to scuba dive, which I had never done before. At the time, I was on the board of directors of the Wayne Westland

YMCA branch. Arrangements were made to hire Bill Rice, the Y's local dive instructor, for a special one-on-one scuba evening class. He was "old school" in his approach to teaching, i.e., slow controlled breathing, underwater neutral balance without a buoyancy compensator vest, plus the necessary homework assignments. Since I would not be able to do a required open water test in Michigan to obtain a diver's certificate prior to my trip, Bill wrote a short "for whom it may concern" letter. It explained what we had covered in the pool and that I had passed all the classwork and was proficient and comfortable with all the equipment.

About midway through the trip, I came to learn that Bob had made a few open water dives in Michigan, and that Bob's friends, Jim and "Big John," were experienced divers and had made several ocean dives. My intimidation of zero experience and frayed nerves grew by the day. We reserved a dive trip with a local scuba company that operated out of Roadtown in Tortola, British Virgin Islands. There were three or four additional divers with different degrees of experience. As we stood next to the dive boat while preparing to leave, Robert, our dive master, started to chat about the dive and to check each person's dive card and their own underwater experiences.

When he got to me, I apprehensively handed him my letter. He frowned and with pursed lips cautiously read the letter twice, then pointing to my three friends asked if I was with them. I nodded yes, and he said, "Okay … but you stay close to me." Off we went.

Our dive journey started with about a 45-minute boat ride to the wreck of the Rhone, a 310' British Royal Mail ship that sunk during a hurricane in October 1867 that killed 123 people. At the wreck's site, the dive master told us to pull ourselves down the anchor line and form a circle at the bottom to wait for him. Excited and nervous, we each sat there giving ourselves the official diver's OK signal and smiling, behind our masks and breathing regulators. I remember thinking, wow, this is really cool. I am sitting on the bottom of the ocean surrounded by beautiful coral amid lots of different meandering fish. Robert arrived last with Big John to complete the circle. As rehearsed earlier on the boat, Robert was going to point to each of us directly with the diver's OK sign. We were to answer back confidently, robustly with a positive OK signal if we were comfortable and ready to proceed. He worked his way around the circle and pointed to each of us. The last one, Big John, wasn't so sure as he waved his hands side to side like he was waving goodbye out of the first-grade school bus window to his mother. Robert didn't hesitate; he took Big John's hand and swam him to the top. When he returned, he checked all our air pressures and motioned us to follow him as he headed to the wreck. We slowly moved deeper into the sea beside the coral reef before stopping near the hull of the Rhone. He pointed to features as we traveled along. After about 25 minutes, we stopped and he made another air supply check, then peeled two divers away including Jim and directed them toward the anchor line and motioned them to swim up.

We then followed Robert down to where the bowsprit still rested next to a big coral formation that was home to hundreds of beautiful fish. After a few more minutes we headed back toward our anchor when Robert paused to check each air gauge before giving the signal to head up. One by one they swam up to the surface until I was alone. Robert looked at my remaining air pressure while tapping it and then looked at me. I gave him a firm OK. He signaled to follow close, except this time he gently weaved his way to about 80 feet down to the jumble of wreckage inside the hull, with me close behind, to a large diameter steel drum that was the Rhone's massive boiler. We dove down and up and through a small opening into the boiler where we were able to stand up inside and into a pocket of air between 12 to 16 inches high. We slipped off our masks to the forehead and held the regulator's mouthpiece in our hand and started to chat. We were there a minute or two when Robert said, "You are an easy breather, and going to be a good diver. It's not that often I get a chance to take someone in here." Boy, was I happy, and feeling super confident. I wore a big grin all the way back to the boat and politely restrained from gloating for the remainder of our trip.

Over the summer Carol and Jerry took a scheduled scuba class from Bill and we all did our open water tests together at an old quarry in St. Clair County and a dive in the St. Clair River near Port Huron. The interesting thing about that dive was that you had to climb down a ladder to the river and while under water you had to hang on to something because of the swift current. When freighters would go by you could hear the props chug chug chug along and see the dark hulls above pass by. Very eerie. Very cool.

Diving was a big part of my life and an important sport for me, with over 100 dives in three oceans, plus many throughout the Caribbean islands and Great Lakes. For Carol's first ocean dive we flew to Grand Cayman, one of the most beautiful dive spots in the world and did our first ocean dive together from a beach located next to a dive shop. Nobody else was around. I told Carol to just follow me and naively I proceeded to guide us down along the ocean bottom. Captured by its beauty, I didn't realize that we were down to over 80 ft! Way too deep for Carol's first dive. We immediately turned back. She did great. The rest of the Cayman dives were with a dive master and other divers. Grand Cayman is noted for its famous wall dives. At first you descend to about 100 ft and then slowly work your way through large, colorful coral formations with schools of various species of fish ending at about 130 feet. A serious dive.

The exciting portion of the dive is when the coral ends and the sea floor abruptly stops. You go over "the wall"; you turn around and look straight down toward the dark 3000 ft floor beneath you.

Occasionally at that depth you need to add some air into your buoyancy compensator vest to keep yourself from sinking. I was sinking. After a few minutes over the wall, I noticed I was looking up several feet to Carol. I had to remove my regulator with my left hand and blow air into my inflator tube with the other. That was my first uncomfortable dive moment. My scuba career ended in 2005 in the Indian Ocean off the coast of South Africa. That dive was the complete opposite of my first dive on the wreck of the Rhone. More on that later.

*   *   *

I obtained press credentials from the *Wayne Eagle* for the April 12 first launch of the space shuttle program from Cape Canaveral, 20 years to the day after Soviet cosmonaut Yuri Gargarin was first to ride a rocket to space. Coincidentally, the shuttle *Columbia* landed two days later on April 14 at Edwards Air Force Base (formally Muroc AFB) where Chuck Yeager broke the sound barrier. Mom and Jerry were able to join me for the 7:00 a.m. liftoff of *Columbia*. It was piloted by *Apollo 16* astronaut John Young and rookie Robert Crippen. I was there in the front row again, maybe not the closest, but front row. It was very exciting, and I was grateful to be a witness to space history again, but frankly, it wasn't close to my experience and the thrill of the *Saturn 5 Apollo 11* launch.

In September, our daughter Joan started college at Michigan State University, my mother and father's alma mater, that proved to be much more emotional than expected. Carol had to drive us home while I pressed my face against the car's side window to hide my tears.

1982's Super Bowl XVI was played at the Silverdome in Pontiac, Michigan. The outside temperature was the coldest on record for any Super Bowl and still is. Vice President George

H.W. Bush, and the usual high rollers and celebrities were in attendance. On a whim I decided to drive to Pontiac from Canton and try to "scalp" a ticket. I was accustomed to doing that for U of M and MSU football games and a number of concerts. I spent 20 or 30 minutes at one of the main gates; it was very windy and extremely cold. Nobody had a ticket to sell. I thought I would try my luck at another entrance on my way back to the car for one last chance. Kickoff was in about 10 minutes, and just as I started to leave, I noticed some dollar bills blowing across the sidewalk and naturally without hesitation I ran after them. It was really cold. By the time I finally recovered four $50 bills, the place was pretty well cleared out.

I was sure my face was frostbitten, and my nose was about to fall off as I started the mile walk back to my car on a side street, when I saw a lone guy walking toward a charter bus, "Have an extra ticket?" I called out.

"Yeah. I do."

"How much do you want for it?"

"I'm not sure, has the game started yet?"

"I'm not sure either." I offered two $50 bills. He took it and I walked into the stadium never turning back. I spent several minutes in the bathroom splashing water on my face and ears, then made my way to my seat on the 20-yard line about 25 rows up. Not bad. I missed the opening kickoff by only a few minutes. The game ended with Joe Montana of San Francisco beating Cincinnati 20 to 16.

When we finished the new Lake House, there was a small dispute between me and the local builder we hired for the project. It was painless and quickly settled when the contractor agreed to my proposition. I resolved then, if in the future I ever did this again, I would be my own general contractor. I hired and negotiated all of the subcontractors; including carpentry, plumbing, heat/air, electric, drywall, decorators, painters, site and infrastructure plus a few others.

On December 10th I surprised Carol with a flight to Los Angeles, California (she thought we were going to Florida to visit her parents). We rented a car for a week and toured most of southern California. One afternoon we stood in line at the NBC studios and got the last two tickets of the taping of Johnny Carson's Christmas show, front row center. Carol's seat was next to the guy holding Johnny's cue cards. During Johnny's monologue, he was looking at the cue cards and Carol. We spent the night at the Ambassador Hotel in Los Angeles where Senator Robert Kennedy was assassinated in 1968 after his California primary victory speech. After dinner we wandered around the hotel and ended up in its large ballroom. No one was around so I led Carol back into the kitchen to see the very spot where Kennedy was shot. That night as we watched the Johnny Carson show on TV, we could hear our own distinct laughter.

On another night we stayed on Cunard's 1936 retired ocean liner *Queen Mary* that was permanently docked at Long Beach, a suburb of Los Angeles. Next to the ship was the infamous Howard Hughes's *Spruce Goose* airplane, that only flew once on a short flight over the nearby bay on November 2, 1947. The behemoth flying machine was the largest propeller plane ever built. It was made from birch and spruce plywood and permanently housed in a huge, guarded, secured dome hangar and was never opened to the public. It was surrounded by a tall chain link fence with barbed wire on top. That night I was just looking around and happened upon an unlocked opening. I casually walked up through some tall weeds and grass to a small door into the massive hangar. I slowly opened the door and took two steps in.

To my surprise I gazed upon the famous eerily brilliantly lit *Spruce Goose*. Suddenly I heard, "Step back out NOW!" from a security guard. With a drawn gun pointed squarely at me, I instinctively raised my hands, from watching cops and robber movies. I didn't even whisper a word, then silently walked backward, left the building, and closed the door behind me and heard the click of a deadbolt. What an unexpected treat. The next few days were spent doing all the tourist highlights. Our last night was spent at the Beverly Hills Hilton Hotel.

*　*　*

On March 18, 1983, son Jon's birthday, we purchased the Harbour Club on Belvedere Avenue, a defunct eight-unit Boat House Condominium project built over Round Lake for approximately $900,000. One of the eight units was finished with furniture and accessories that was used as a model. The other seven were rough framed in. The purchase price also included enough frontage on Round Lake for 10 more residential units and a boat slip marina.

I can remember one night on the *Paper Clipper* in 1978 when we tied up for the evening at what would become the Harbour Club and was thinking how neat it was. Wondering what they were going to do here? We left early the next morning, thinking someone would come around and want us to pay for docking fees before they kicked us out. Providence is amazing. Just 39 years old. How is this possible?

It took some finance ingenuity to acquire the Harbour Club—a trait I was really starting to enjoy. Finding pieces of an imaginary puzzle without borders and making adjustments as needed to create a lasting landmark. There were several parties of interest that needed to be addressed and satisfied before we could obtain a construction loan with Mr. Michael. The previous developer's bank in Saginaw, various liens and the underlying titled property owner Doug Bathey, a businessman from Plymouth, Michigan, who summered in Charlevoix at his home on Round Lake across from the Harbour Club, had to be cleaned up.

Most of the infrastructure was complete. To finish the other units and get them ready for the trades to start (plumbing/heating, electric, drywall, etc.), I hired two local carpenters, Les Petersen and Brandon LaBlanc. Les was a smart nice guy in his late 60s and taught me a lot of practical solutions to the many unique and unforeseen issues that came from trying to convert a huge land-mark boathouse over water and garages into eight residential con-dominium units. Brandon was a beer drinker with a laugh that could be heard around the lake. He left at "beer thirty" every day no matter what, even in the middle of his hammer backswing. I hired and coordinated all the trades and was at the job every day from 8:00 a.m. until whenever.

We had sold our unit at the Lake House to John Upjohn, one of the heirs to the pharmaceutical giant "Upjohn" in Kalamazoo, which years later merged into Pfizer. In June, Carol and I, Jenifer and Jessica moved into unit #7, the top-floor end apartment over the water as our new summer home. We hired Linda Mason, a local interior designer whose mother happened to be one of my mother's best friends from Redford, Michigan.

Phase one: Harbour Club over Round Lake.

When six of eight units were sold at the Harbour Club, we began making plans for Phase II which required site approval from the City Planning, Zoning, and the Charlevoix City Council. Most of the sub-contractors we used to trim out the first Phase were ready and willing to continue working for me on Phase II, but I needed to find a builder with a big enough experienced carpenter crew. After a few interviews with local builders, Jack Begrow suggested I call Richard Wilbur from Petoskey. He was a general contractor who typically ran and profited a job from the ground up, with a crew of six or seven men, including Rod Hickman as leader and Peter Schwartzfischer, his son-in-law, and son John. After touring the project site, Dick and I continued our discussion with a three-hour lunch. I must have alleviated some doubt he may have had with my ability to be the general contractor for such a big job. Instinct told me that he was the right choice, and he was. We worked together on various projects for over 15 years. A good man. We usually had lunch together on Fridays when we discussed an assortment of job issues. I can still recall his smile while telling me, "Any profit, Jon, is better than a loss." And often I would hear, "Worrying, Jon, will only get you one step closer to the grave." Another fortuitous encounter with a mentor and a man of character with a patient demeanor. Fate.

In the early days of 1984, I was able to cajole two more, and the last press passes from the Wayne Eagle. In the very early morning of February 11, Carol joined me to witness the first space shuttle landing at Cape Canaveral's 15,000-foot-long, 16-inch-thick reinforced concrete runway. As we waited next to the landing strip in dew-covered unkempt grasses, we heard the famous double "BANG" from the broken sound barrier of the nose and tail on the one-hundred-ton goliath glider; it silently approached the waiting crowd before touching down and rolling to a stop just a few hundred feet in front of us. Another close-up eyewitness to America's space history.

* * *

Signs of my first "mid-life" crisis appeared during my 40's … right on schedule, when I bought a new, bright red 944 Porsche sports car for $23,800 from the Bill Cook Dealership in Farmington Hills with the proceeds of a defunct Office World. Carol dropped me off at the dealer and I followed her to Canton slipping and sliding most of the way in a light snowfall. I kept the car for 25 years, coincidentally selling it in Florida on the same month and day that I bought it.

Also, in 1984 I formed a new partnership with Steve Michael (49%), whose father was a prominent attorney in Charlevoix to start another office supply business. Steve was an MSU graduate who worked for us as a painter at Harbour Club. I named it H.M. Nickels, while Steve researched a location that suggested Charlotte, North Carolina, was the best chance for success. I found a source to make up thousands of imprinted wooden nickels to promote the new store. That Easter Sunday, Carol, Jen, and Jessica drove with me to Charlotte. We made a side trip to Mammoth Cave. Then we stopped at Sergeant York's gravesite in Tennessee. He was a famous World War I hero whose biography and movie I liked. York received a Congressional Medal of Honor and is buried in Pall Mall, Tennessee. The hero's grave looked forlorn and forgotten. Even the brave and the famous are quickly forgotten. Over my lifetime of travel, Carol has accompanied me to hundreds of historical or notorious gravesites throughout the United States and world. A little weird but interesting. We then continued through the Great Smoky Mountains before arriving at the new H.M. Nickels store. Jon C was already there helping with the assembly and layout of the new merchandise displays. After a few years Steve closed Nickels and returned to Charlevoix.

One fine day in the summer of '84, the Presidential yacht, the

USS *Sequoia*, came to Charlevoix and stayed at the Harbour Club seawall. It was a beautiful 104-foot, 1925 classic wood boat complete with presidential history from Herbert Hoover to Jimmy Carter. Carter unfortunately sold it in a recession as a token of fiscal responsibility. That was very irresponsible. Carol and the girls joined me for a personal tour and on another eventful fine day that summer, a 1962 57' Chris-Craft Constellation "Connie" motor yacht tied up to our dock. It was also an oversized beautiful wood boat. The owners were Michael and Lois Farmer from Rockford, Michigan. While we toured Unit 5 in Phase 1, I sensed that this guy could sell ice to an Eskimo. That evening Mike invited Carol and me to the Argonne Supper Club on Boyne City Road, for its famous shrimp dinners. Being from the suburbs of Detroit, Carol and I never acquired much of a taste for fish and none at all for shrimp. When Mike found out we were 40 years old and had never eaten shrimp and were in no rush to start, he was flabbergasted. Mike challenged us to try it. Well … by the end of the evening we were on our second bottle of wine and a second helping of Argonne's Famous Shrimp and have enjoyed eating shrimp since.

The next morning, Mike approached me at the job and wanted to negotiate the price on Unit 5. I told him that we don't negotiate a published price of a condominium, but that I'm always ready to work with a buyer in some limited form or fashion.

It reminded me of selling desks at Parkway Office Supply. More than once a customer would be looking for a deal on a desk, and I would usually say, "No, I can't sell you this desk for the price you want, but I do have a 'like new' desk in the back that I could let you have at a slight discount." Sold! I can't remember how many times I ran to the back room to empty my desk onto the floor, while the customer waited to load it onto a truck or into a station wagon. I usually sold my chair too.

After I told Mike I couldn't adjust the price, he asked if Carol and I would like to go through the 57' Connie. Wondering who was the seller here? Well … after he guided us from bow to stern, top to bottom, we ended at the helm station when he fired up the two big 12-cylinder Detroit Diesel engines that purred like a fat king lion after eating a gazelle. I took his boat as a down payment on Unit 5. Carol couldn't believe it! I couldn't believe it either.

It was the Saturday of the 1984 Venetian Festival, and it was suggested that we enter the evening's Venetian parade that night. I walked over to the Chamber of Commerce office and told Jackie Merta, my friend and chamber president, that I just bought a big wood boat. I asked if it was too late to get in the parade that night. She said, "Sure Jon, we'd love to have you, and as a matter of fact with a classic yacht like that we'd like you to lead the parade." We renamed the *Farmhouse* to *Phase III* (a tie-in and continuum of Harbour Club Phases I, II, and now Phase III). With Mike by my side, along with a boatload of family and friends, we led the evening's light parade as I maneuvered the giant in front of thousands of cheering East Park spectators.

Phase III in Lake Charlevoix.

We won first place in the classic division. What a boat. What an expensive boat to keep in pristine ship-shape condition. Mike and I remained friends, and a few years later, he bought a rental house we had on Park Avenue, and I bought a car from him. Yes, he could sell ice to an Eskimo and coal to a Kentuckian, and a big wood boat to a foolish fool.

We had planned for an August 1st family cruise on *Phase III* to Northport and Leland for our last family trip together before son Jon got married. The family memory on this occasion was while leaving Charlevoix for the first time on the 57' Connie, the harbor was still full of boats left over from Venetian week. As a boater family for many years, my first and most important rule for crew and captain is to never ever raise your voice or scream during times of trouble or pending trouble or trouble itself; chaos begets accidents. As I pulled out of the dock at the Harbour Club that morning, we decided to tow the antique classic wood dinghy that came with the boat. We thought it might be of use in one of the harbors, or at least we could show off the beautiful handmade dory.

While we were in the middle of Round Lake waiting for the 10:00 a.m. bridge opening, surrounded by boats doing the same, I had to alternate idle and slow forward maneuvers against the current and surrounding boat traffic. As the bridge operator signaled with the one long, one short horn blast to announce the bridge opening, I reversed the engines to keep a safe distance from all the forward boats. Then, suddenly my children came up to me and calmly said, "Dad you just ran over the dinghy. What!" I screamed. "Why didn't you tell me!" I yelled, running back to assess the damage and saw the crippled dinghy, partially submerged and circled with splinters of wood. Now everyone on the boat is screaming and hollering at one another to avoid the curse of guilt, while the spectators on the other boats stared at us, as they carefully passed us by, toward the opened bridge. After conditions calmed down and with the dinghy still partially afloat, we slowly made our way back to our dock. I put on my scuba gear and dove under to cut the tightly wound tow line from one of *Phase III's* propeller shafts. A group of us lifted the mangled dinghy remains onto the dock.

We finally made it to Leland, Michigan, later that afternoon. Bill Martin, my first customer of Harbour Club, eventually sliced the dinghy in half and made it into a beautiful salad and shrimp bar for the Weathervane Restaurant.

Bill Johnson, a U of M professor and celebrated landscape architect, sailed into Charlevoix and spent a few nights at our marina. I toured the project with him and his wife, Nancy. They expressed an interest, so I naturally gave him some sales information when he mentioned that he knew of Jack Begrow. He told me that he was sailing to Traverse City and then heading back to his office in Ann Arbor and may be back in a couple of weeks. A few days later, Jack told me how respected and world-famous Bill was. Bill was a thinking, soft spoken, benignant man who became my friend. By late August, the Johnsons bought Unit 6 at the Harbour Club along with a boat slip. The following summer he gave us a beautiful colored pencil drawing of the completed Harbour Club project, as viewed from his sailboat on Round Lake, it's still hanging on my wall.

*   *   *

On August 18, 1984, son Jon married his high school sweetheart, Regina Chapman, in Ypsilanti's Methodist Church before dancing the night away at Eastern Michigan's faulty air-conditioned Welch Hall.

We sold out Phase I by the end of that first summer including our own, Unit 7, and had taken reservation agreements on some of the 10 units in Phase II. We found ourselves living onboard *Phase*

III. About this time, a project was presented to the Charlevoix City Council for a hotel on Round Lake by a downstate developer next to the bridge where the Charlevoix Lumber Co. had operated for close to a century. The only thing I can recall when I saw the plan in the *Charlevoix Courier* newspaper was that all the parking seemed to be on the water side, so that the view to Round Lake from your room was interrupted by a parking lot full of cars. We stayed on *Phase III* until October when Bill Johnson knocked on the window and said, "Get your things together Jon, I want you to rent our condominium for the winter." So we did. That winter we stored *Phase III* inside Walstrom Marine in Harbor Springs; at the time they were the closest marina that had a lift big enough to handle her.

The proposed hotel project across the lake was eventually abandoned and the property was presented to me as a possible opportunity. Jim Hiller, a relative of my stepmother, Darleen Williams Hisey, had owned and operated the lumberyard on the property for many years before selling it to a downstate big shot newspaper publisher, and presidential political appointee, John McGoff. He had collected various properties around the area including the Beaver Island Boat Company and knew my dad through *The Wayne Dispatch.*

* * *

As we were finishing Phase II construction and sales at the Harbour Club, I began to think more about the project across the lake, buoyed by almost five years of a lucky success run. I can recall sitting alone late at night and into the next day at the dinette table on *Phase III,* doing several spreadsheets with an old Victor adding machine from Parkway of different income and expense scenarios based on hypothetical square footages. After a few lonesome nights of this, and hours of thinking, talking, listening, and imagining, I decided to go for it. Edgewater Inn was the project of my life, and the one that permanently changed the landscape and tenor of downtown Charlevoix and its harbor. It was one of the earlier hotel condominium concept projects "purpose built" in northwestern Michigan.

Once again, a call went out to see if Mr. Michael was willing and able to provide an acquisition/first building construction loan for the first phase, but this time the upfront loan amount at risk would be over $1,000,000. During the initial phone call, Mr. Michael suggested that amount could present a problem, but if I could start with a request of $950,000 with increases as the development progressed, he said the bank could probably make it happen.

A few years later during a *Detroit News* press interview regarding the hotel condominium concept and specifically Edgewater Inn, the reporter asked me about my background and the development business. I briefly explained to her how my wife and I started a small office supply business fifteen years ago with our last $500 selling paper and pencils in the Wayne/Westland, Michigan, area. I continued to tell her about the short history of the development business with no partners and no employees that led up to the Edgewater Inn project. She seemed dazzled and asked, "What on earth compelled you to take on such a huge risk?"

"Well," I said after a long thoughtful pause, "*I knew I was smart enough to do it ... and dumb enough to try.*"

*   *   *

That winter Carol and I loaned Clark Block and Supply $50,000 to help J.D. delay an eminent bank foreclosure due to a large investment for a new state-of-the-art block machine that happened to start production just a few months before a severe economic recession. I was briefly involved to facilitate a bank proposal and reorganization plan to help create a pathway into and out of bankruptcy. J.D., myself, and a few others met with attorneys and bankers over several weeks. Within a year Clark Block was reorganized and out of bankruptcy. Shortly thereafter J.D. sent us a $50,000 check plus interest and to his credit, within a few years he paid back all the agreed to forgiven debt.

On December 8th Carol and I flew to Aruba for a week's scuba vacation with Jerry and his wife, Nancy. I can remember this trip because during a shore dive with a new friend that I met on the airplane and a guide I met on the beach, we were swimming along the side of a beautiful coral reef, about 60 feet deep. Minding my own business enjoying the moment, a huge eel about three feet away, poked his overinflated, football-sized head from his hidden lair from within the coral. His mouth was wide open and full of large sharp looking teeth, scaring me half to death. I threw up into my regulator's mouthpiece. I was able to maintain a sense of normalcy by removing the mouthpiece and blowing it clear with the oxygen tank and spitting out the remainder of the you-know-what into the ocean. It was bigger than huge!

January 1985 started with me driving to Lansing (Williamston) to sign a binding purchase agreement with John McGoff for the Edgewater Inn property. A token amount of cash provided us with time to go through laborious procedures and protocols to secure all of the necessary permits from the City, the County, the Health Dept., the Michigan DNR, and the US Corps of Engineers before the big risk became real. Edgewater Inn was a huge project not just for me but also for the city and the local townspeople. During the public forums and newspaper coverage, there was a lot of negative opposition that was expected but nevertheless regrettable.

On February 27, Don and Sally Berlage, Rik and Kim

Lobenherz, and Carol and I drove to Parkway Office Supply's parking lot and loaded up it's large cargo delivery truck with our ski equipment and luggage. We sat on the floor amongst our gear as best we could while Jon C drove us to Detroit Metro Airport to start a 10-day ski holiday in Europe. It was everyone's first trip over the Atlantic except Sally and mine. We traveled to and skied Germany, Austria, Switzerland, Italy, and France. On the flight over, bad weather forced our plane to divert to Frankfurt, Germany, causing all our tentative plans to be shuffled and rearranged. We decided to rent a station wagon to drive to the different ski areas. We had no itinerary, plans, or reservations, just Sally's guidebook. By the time Don, Rik, and I left the car rental office, we ended up with a Mercedes Marco Polo Class C camper van. We stowed the skis and poles upright in the bathroom shower and the rest of the gear over the front cab bunk. Off we went, driving, skiing, eating, and drinking our way through Europe's mountains and world-famous ski resorts. A fantastic trip with many memories.

*   *   *

On July 28, I departed Charlevoix on *Phase III* with Carol, Mom, Jon C., Jenifer, and Jessica to Tobermory, Ontario, for scuba diving, with stops at Mackinac Island, Cedarville, Detour Harbor, Meldrum Bay, Little Current, Mary Ann's Cove, and Killarney. We then motored south onto Tobermory at the northern tip of the Bruce Peninsula in Georgian Bay. While there, Carol and family switched places with Jerry, and friends Rik, Steve Michael, and Steve Savoie and his friend. We dove the local wrecks of the Tobermory Canadian Marine Park in clear, frigid 45-degree waters in full wet suits with a dive master as our guide. Besides diving, there is a peculiar tangent anecdote of that trip. *Phase III* was a head turner and was so big we had to dock at the main pier next to the Marina's office and close to town. Our boat became a celebrity of sorts to the local town folk.

On our last night we were strolling back to the boat after a pizza and beer dinner when we noticed several people milling around *Phase III*. As we walked up to the boat, my brother Jerry pretended to be a bystander and spoke to us by saying, "Wow, what a neat boat!"

He then climbed up to the aft deck and said to us and the locals, "Hey, I'm going to see if I can find some beer! Come on up." The crowd began hollering, "You can't do that! Get off of that boat now. Somebody call the police!" I tried to calm everybody down as we all got back on the boat. "It's all right everyone. I'm the owner of the boat. Everything is fine. Have a nice evening." Just as Jerry arrived back on the deck with his hands loaded with cans of cold beer, we could see the flashing lights of the Canadian police cars. Some of the locals started waving to them. Jerry, for some reason (he never could explain), shouted, "Cops!" then jumped off onto the dock and started running. Oh, my God.

I had no registration or MC boat numbers, no bill of sale, no evidence of ownership. After recording all of our driver's licenses, showing our diving gear and a thorough search of the boat and advising them we planned to leave early the next day, the Royal Canadian Police left us, followed by a questioning crowd of good Canadian citizens. Jerry finally reappeared awhile later saying, "That was fun … wasn't it?"

Later that month I drove to Lake St. Clair with Bill Martin to help him bring back his "new" old 1964, 42' wood boat to Charlevoix via Port Austin and Mackinac City. My bunk mate on the trip was Bruce Patterson from Oakland County, a prominent Republican who would later run for Michigan Governor and Attorney General before serving seven terms as Oakland County's Chief Executive.

* * *

One evening after dinner at the Weathervane with Jack Begrow and Bill Johnson, we started conversing about a name for the old lumberyard property. It wasn't long before Bill or I said in unison Waters Edge and then almost immediately we said together Edgewater … Edgewater Inn. Bill Johnson designed Edgewater Inn's exterior concept with a complete set of elevation drawings. Jack followed with all of the construction drawings, and I hired a structural engineering firm from Traverse City to affirm and endorse the project's specifications for the county's Building Department.

We purchased #5 Thistle Downs, an Earl Young home on the north side of Round Lake next to the future Edgewater Inn, for $175,000, with $75,000 down and a$100,000 land contract; we immediately started remodeling with some of Dick Wilbur's crew.

Our Earl Young Thistle Downs home on Round Lake.

On October 18, 1985, after all the governmental approvals, Mr. Michael and I met at attorney Don Berlage's office with several other men dressed in suits who represented monetary interests in the property. I was dressed in the same outfit that I have worn almost every workday for the past 20 years: a heavily starched blue button-down 100% cotton oxford Brooks Brothers shirt with tan khakis and loafers. After the usual pleasantries, we seated ourselves around a big conference table. Mr. Michael opened his briefcase and handed me a sheaf of papers and said, "Before we start, I think Jon should sign the loan application that I have filled out for him." Everyone laughed. That's an example of the mutual trust and rapport Mr. Michael and I had for each other. At the end of the closing, I explained to Mr. Michael that we were having an official groundbreaking ceremony, complete with a silver spade, and local newspapers and public officials at the site. I asked, "Would you like to join us?" With a snap of his closing briefcase and a wink of his eye, he said, "No thanks Jon; let them think you paid cash." Hats off to Mr. Michael.

Breaking Ground for Edgewater Inn.

* * *

On January 26, 1986, Carol and I flew to St. Thomas and the British Virgin Islands. Two days later we were snorkeling on Trunk Bay Beach, St. John's, US Virgin Islands, when the space shuttle *Challenger* exploded just 73 seconds after liftoff, taking with it its seven crew members including Christa McAuliffe, NASA's first and only civilian astronaut, a schoolteacher from New Hampshire. On the 31st we took our first seaplane flight from St. Thomas, an adventure in itself as the plane's windows seemed to be underwater for a few moments before being airborne to St. Croix, US Virgin Islands, to look at real estate options.

In the spring, Gordon Wellman, president of the Charlevoix County State Bank, called me from out of the blue to arrange a meeting to discuss the Weathervane Restaurant. It was currently being leased to and operated by two brothers as Ricardi's Italian Restaurant. In his corner office on Bridge St. and Clinton, Wellman explained how the bank had acquired ownership of the Weathervane property through a loan default. The liquor liability laws had recently changed, and the bank could now be held responsible in the event a patron of the restaurant was overserved alcohol and subsequently involved in an accident. The bank's "deep pockets" could ultimately be liable for millions of dollars above and beyond available insurances. After some questions and answers, he outlined a very good proposal to me to purchase the real estate. It was a generous sweetheart deal. I couldn't believe it, no money and extremely low risk. Like the office supply and the development business, we knew nothing about the food and beverage business; it was someone else's original thought or idea.

I mentioned the meeting and the offer to Bill Martin at the evening's happy hour and mentioned that even though it was practically failsafe, I was hesitant because we were in the middle of Edgewater's first construction phase. The next day Bill came over to the job site and said he was interested in the proposal as a 50/50 partnership, with me as president. Within the hour I called Gordon and bought the Weathervane property and all of the improvements for $350,000, with a 20-year fixed interest mortgage with no down payment. Ricardi's monthly lease payments were enough to pay principal and interest and all expenses. That was easy.

Weathervane Restaurant.

Coincidentally, I had begun conversations with Mr. Bathey about buying the property along Pine River Lane contiguous for several hundred feet to the west side of the Weathervane Restaurant along the channel. I soon bought it with Bill to satisfy and conclude my negotiations with the City for additional off-site parking for the Edgewater Inn's proposed conference center, and to benefit the Weathervane Restaurant. About a year later I donated, with Bill's consent, the property to the City of

Charlevoix with the condition that it would forever remain in its natural state.

This was not easy. After about a year and a half, Bill started to get restless. Just being a passive landlord in Charlevoix's iconic restaurant building was not enough. He started complaining about Ricardi's operation, food, and service. His idea was to terminate the lease and for us to become the active operators and managers and bring back the Weathervane name to its previous splendor and traditions. So … my risk-free sweetheart deal now became all risk.

After another 2½ years of running the restaurant, Bill and I each had close to $100,000 in lost operating expenses, and the stress on both of our families was becoming an untenable burden. Some of Bill's children and Carol, Joan, and Jenifer (Jessica was only 12) all pitched in to help. Something had to be done. The Charlevoix Rotary Club had their weekly lunch meetings downstairs at the Weathervane. One day after their meeting, Bob Kern, a friend and local realtor, saw me upstairs and asked if I would be interested in getting another operator for the restaurant. "Possibly," I said, trying to hold back my look of desperation and hope.

The next week I found myself sitting around a coffee table in a soft pastel chintz easy chair at the Bay View Inn in Petoskey talking to Stafford Smith and Dudley Marvin, president and vice president of Stafford's Hospitality. It was a great meeting. Stafford reminisced about working at the Weathervane in the 1950s when Earl Young operated it and had his real estate and construction office downstairs. I began to express my enthusiasm for their interest and offered some extemporaneous possibilities of daily structure and terms. I think I may have caught them off guard and after some good discussions they said that they would talk it over and get back to me as they stood up, signaling the meeting was over.

I stayed seated. Puzzled, Stafford asked, "Is there anything else, Jon?" I said, "Yes, I'd like to continue this and see if we can conclude with an outline of a gentleman's agreement." They both said they had other places to be. I responded, "Well, I would appreciate it if I could wait here for you because … I'm not leaving." Smiling, each gave me a questionable look as they sat back down. About an hour later we were having tuna salad sandwiches and iced tea in the shade of the back porch dining room. We ended the lunch with a handshake agreement. Over the next few weeks and after numerous discussions with their attorneys, we went from that handshake to a few dozen pages of legalese that explained the principles and mechanics of our original meeting. Bill and our mutual families were delighted. That chance call from the bank and its offer to me resulted in a nice part of my retirement income. Fate?

"It is not the contract you sign. It is the hand that you shake." —JAH

---

* * *

In the spring of 1986, we took a ski trip to Vail with the entire family and rented a large house in the Potato Patch neighborhood with great views of Vail Mountain. Astronaut John Glenn owned a home nearby. One day Carol and I took a day off from skiing and started looking for a ski vacation condominium. Eventually settling on the "Charter in Beaver Creek," a ski in/ski out, two-suite, high-end hotel/condominium for $245,000. It was a relatively new mountain resort developed close to and operated by Vail. One of its claims to fame was that President Gerald Ford owned a vacation home there that included a detached indoor lap swimming pool. You could see a portion of the house and most of the pool building from a chairlift ride that skirted the property.

Phase III was a classic beautiful boat but, unfortunately, very expensive to maintain, so after three seasons we decided to sell her. Over the summer I negotiated an agreement to trade an Edgewater Inn balcony unit for a new 1987 39' Sea Ray Express from Brennan Marine in Bay City. Yes, I did it again, but this boat was an even trade, and as of this writing our family is still making memories with it over 36 years later.

And so it was, that on a gorgeous early fall day Carol and I started our trip on *Phase III* to Bay City where we were going to lay up the boat for the winter with hopes of Brennan selling it. As we approached the Straits of Mackinac near the abandoned lighthouse, I came down with a massive headache. I didn't normally get headaches, but this one was extremely painful and debilitating. As soon as we tied up in Mackinaw City Marina, I called J.J. Johnson, a friend who operated the Best Western Motel in Mackinaw City and told him of my condition and that we needed a room. Within minutes JJ arrived and helped us tie up while I told the marina's harbormaster that we would be back in a few days. JJ went above and beyond the call of duty as we spent the rest of the day nursing my pain in a comped deluxe suite with a pink heart-shaped bathtub. The next morning Mom, Jenifer, and Jessica drove up to get us.

Oddly enough, two days later a lady who saw our for-sale sign on *Phase III* while taking a walk in the marina called. We came to terms very quickly and she told me that a professional captain was going to pick up the boat and bring it back to Muskegon where it was going to be kept. Wow, what good luck. Over the phone I explained to her the idiosyncrasies of an old wood boat and also wrote a page of instructions of operations for the captain and new owner. I placed it on the helm next to the steering wheel in plain sight when Carol and I went up to retrieve our personal belongings and say our goodbyes to the classy boat.

A few days later, I received a call from the buyer of the boat, informing me that *Phase III* had floundered in Lake Michigan just before reaching Muskegon and that the captain had sent out a distress May Day call in rough seas because the boat was on the brink of sinking. The Coast Guard came to the rescue and started pumping out the bilge with two massive pumps while apparently a helicopter retrieved the captain. The boat was stabilized and towed into Muskegon Harbor. Wow, unbelievable. I knew right away that the captain did not follow my instructions and never once visually checked the bilge or manually turned on the pump switch, as I had advised both verbally and in writing. An old wooden boat and he never looked. Not very professional! About a week later I received a certified letter addressed to me from then-Michigan Governor Frank Kelly's office. The lady we sold the boat to was the head of the Michigan Department of Maritime Safety. The letter demanded $5,000 for recovery expenses and stress. I sent a certified check the next day. Bizarre, to say the least. Not so lucky.

One particular getaway I recall was in 1986 when Carol and I flew to Tucson, Arizona, on a last-minute whim with free airline voucher tickets. Over the years, whenever I flew either alone or with family, my job as a ticket agent for Northwest Airlines gave me insight on the reservation system of overbooking flights. It allowed me to accumulate dozens of free "bump" ticket vouchers by volunteering to wait for the next available flight, and that sometimes included an upgrade to first class. We picked up some brochures of things to do and rented a car as soon as we arrived in Tucson. We ended up at Tanque Verde horse Dude Ranch about 30 miles out of town in the desert. On the first day a horse wrangler looked me over in my khaki pants and starched blue button-down shirt and asked me, "What kind of experience do you new cowboys have with horses?" We spent the rest of the day in a single file, bringing up the rear, walking my horse named

Penelope, and following Carol and the rest of the new dudes between the tall, thorny Saguaro cactus.

The next morning when asked about my equestrian knowledge of horses, I said, "I have lots of experience, put me down as an expert. Heck, I practically grew up on a horse, and by the way my wife owned her own horse named Champ as a child." About an hour later on my new horse named Dynamite, Carol and I were in a full gallop through a shallow winding stream whooping and hollering, waving one hand with my ball cap and the other with a slight cowboy grip on the reins. I turned my head over my shoulder and shouted to Carol, "This is fantastic, how fun, yippee I aye!" Dynamite exploded and with one buck threw me clear off the saddle head over heels and onto the soft wet sand of the riverbank. No harm—I remounted quickly with a bruised ego and a lot of liability release paperwork back at the barn. That night as we sat around the campfire enjoying steak dinners and drinks with our fellow cowboys and cowgirls, my embarrassing experience on the trail was the evening's topic.

During November 21 to December 4, I returned to Road Town in the British Virgin Islands along with Carol, Jenifer, and Jessica, and rented a 44' two-masted Ketch sailboat named "Happy Heart" from Hugh and Heidi Griffin, hotel owners I knew in Traverse City. We cruised, snorkeled, and anchored out around the islands for a week under the clear Caribbean evening sky. Lots of fun, lots of adventure, and near mishaps that we talked and laughed about for years.

In 1986, the Fox Broadcasting Co. began as an alternative to the "big three" networks (ABC, CBS, and NBC). A separate division, called Fox News, began broadcasting in 1996 as an alternate cable news channel. It eventually and unfortunately, facilitated and exacerbated the conservative far right-wing control of *my* Republican Party. It stimulated a portion of our citizens to resentment and tribalism; that eventually coalesced into cultural paranoia. I read somewhere and came to believe that humans are hardwired to believe what they are told by other human beings who they perceive to be like themselves, or like they may wish to be. It leads to idolization, or be easily conned by a celebrity. Citizens being swayed by the faint winds of an irrational whim.

Beware of loud-speaking priests, politicians, and potentates. Lies and fear need to be loud. Truth, kindness, and love need only a whisper. —JAH

In 1987, England and France agreed to build a 32-mile tunnel under the English Channel connecting the British Isles to Europe. Each country started digging from their side of the channel and somewhere 150 feet below the channel's seabed they met within inches of each other. Several years later Carol and I with our daughters took a train between France and England. Spooky. Another engineering marvel in a single lifetime.

The first two weeks of March were spent skiing with family in Beaver Creek and Vail, while staying at our new Charter Condominium #2435/40. My highlight of skiing memories over many years was standing on top of a mountain's ski run and yelling to my family as I started to move, "OK guys … follow me!" It was only a few years before some of my family had to wait at the bottom of the chairlift line for me to catch up. In April, I flew solo back to Beaver Creek to ski with Jack and Barb Begrow at the Charter (I would trade condo time for architectural services). Barb couldn't ski anymore because of her arthritis.

During this particular trip, my skiing style changed from as many fast turns as possible, some called me wiggle hips, to High-speed cruising with accentuated graceful long sweeping turns. Jack and I traded the lead skiing down the Centennial run from the very top nonstop to the very bottom, estimated to be three miles long. Our legs felt like Jell-O and hurt like they were in the jaws of a big vice. That was tough, and we did it again, several agains. I relished high-speed cruising with my family for the rest of my skiing days.

Later that year I flew alone to Miami and rented a car and meandered down to Key West and back to look at real estate, and to think. Then a few weeks later Carol joined me in the Keys to revisit potential property that was interesting. While in Key West, my island of choice and author Ernest Hemingway's home with his second wife Paula, I purchased a First Edition autographed copy of Hemingway's *For Whom the Bell Tolls*. It eventually became the centerpiece of my Hemingway and other First Edition book collection.

By the end of 1987, I formed Carriage Club Investments, a partnership with Rik Lobenherz (15%), to purchase the Chicago Club storage building that was used to store horses, carriages, and later automobiles on Cherry Street across from the municipal tennis courts. We wanted to convert the historically significant garage into eight condominiums. The neighboring citizens stopped the project, and the landmark was regrettably demolished before selling the property to a third party. I was disappointed that the city did not have the respect for some of its historical structures.

* * *

In the spring, I visited Jack and Barb Begrow at a cottage they rented on the island of Virgin Gorda, British Virgin Islands. It was located across a one-lane pathway that led to the island's iconic boulder "Baths." During the stay Jack and I took the ferry over to Road Town, Tortola, to meet with local architect Michael Helm who was an acquaintance of Jack's. Michael had reached out to him while searching for an investor to help develop some beachfront property that he had owned for several years. It was located about three miles from the center of Road Town and was historically known as Kingstown.

Since my first visit to the British Virgin Islands in 1980, I was hooked. I loved it all and could see myself naturally assimilate into the casual T-shirt, laid-back island time (no watches) lifestyle. I was smitten by everything I saw and everybody I met. At 44 years old, I was ready to pursue the life of a waking living dream. Maybe not a beach bum but close. Family and the exciting adventures of business kept me occupied.

Within a month of long-distance phone calls and faxing (sending copies through phone lines), a partnership was created between me at 50% interest, and Michael Helm and Colin Evans, Michael's business partner from Sao Paulo, Brazil. Colin was familiar with island construction and had a history of logistics, budget pricing, and of monitoring a project's progress. Because of the US tax laws, I opened an escrow account of $50,000 with me or my local BVI solicitor (attorney) David Raworth as the only signatories.

That winter the three of us rendezvoused in Toronto, Canada, to meet with a group from the Bank of Nova Scotia. The partnership had agreed with my financing plan that called for an initial bank construction line of credit for $500,000 collateralized by the beachfront property and the "Kingstown Beach Inn" partnership. The safety clause that I insisted on with Colin and Michael, and that I included in our presentation to the bank, was that no money would be drawn down against the loan until four of the six units of the first building phase were reserved with binding contracts and deposits.

Later, on my second and solo trip to Toronto, I obtained a letter of intent from the bank that outlined them as the lender of record and that the original authorized amount was to be $500,000 with the agreed-to terms. Michael told me later that it was the first time an international bank was willing to lend money for a hotel condominium in the British Virgin Islands.

On one of my visits to Road Town, I remember a meeting that Michael had arranged with the island's elected prime minister, whose name was Roosevelt. He was a large, black native islander with a big smile and easy laugh who during the initial small talk told us that his daughter happened to attend the Interlochen Music Camp in Traverse City, Michigan. I thought to myself that's cool; this is going to be good. After Mike and I showed him our plans and ideas and discussed typical questions and answers, he suggested that he liked it. He said (or implied) it would be beneficial for the project if we would contribute $50,000 toward construction of a new elementary school that he wanted to build near the west end of the island. While walking back to Mike's office, he said, "Shit! I didn't see that coming."

Amidst a lot of interest and inquiries about the new beachfront project located within the British Virgin Islands, we got two signed contracts relatively quickly and solid leads from the St. Thomas realtor I had hired. Brochures were printed, polo shirts were handed out, kitchen cabinets and furniture were decided on and priced out with shipping from Miami to Road Town. Colin's preliminary detailed cost projections were within our original working estimates.

It's a good thing I didn't give away all my winter clothes. Friction between Jack and Mike, and Colin's and my frustration with Mike stalled the project and then it fizzled into a chronic state of comatose.

Several months later, Michael and Colin called me and said they had a wealthy buyer from Pennsylvania for my side of the partnership. He did not require a presale condition before construction could start. They informed me he was willing to pay a nice bonus for my half. I said, "OK, with the stipulation that the bonus would be applied to the purchase of a unit in the first phase priced at cost, plus be reimbursed for any monies spent from my initial escrow account." We all agreed. At least I got my money back. A major disappointment. A life-changing regret. No fate, no luck, no shit.

In 2000, I returned to Tortola with Carol, Jenifer, granddaughter Julia, and brother Jerry to begin a sailing trip and drove out to my dream. Nothing. Just a broken faded sign, "Future Site of Kingstown Beach Inn." My lasting hunch is that Michael and Colin were good men and returned my investment knowing the project's future was becoming doubtful.

In the late fall of 1988, I graduated from the Dale Carnegie course in Stafford's Perry Hotel in Petoskey with an invitation to be an assistant teacher. I thanked them but declined. As much as I enjoyed the class, I remained very shy and hesitant to extemporaneous public speaking.

*　*　*

In 1989, I formed a partnership with architects Pat and Carol Jackson from Ann Arbor who had a home on the north side of Round Lake. We named it Bridge Street Properties and purchased the Leuthauser's Restaurant building (218 Bridge St.) in the middle of downtown. A few years later I wanted to expand the project; that caused Pat some discomfort, and he asked to be bought out. Soon after, I reached an agreement with Bill Supernaw, the owner of the old Charlevoix Cinema movie theater adjacent to Leuthauser's. The next challenge was to negotiate an arduous and complex real estate transfer to develop and build the new Cinema III Theater on Antrim St. I then combined the two Bridge Street properties and developed Harbour Plaza, a four-unit commercial and five residential condominiums overlooking Round Lake.

That summer Carol and I departed Charlevoix for one of our many trips on *Engenuity* to the North Channel, Ontario, Canada;

some were taken with children, grandchildren, and friends. Over the span of more than 36 years and counting, *Engenuity* became our clan's "summer cottage." It has provided us with hundreds of wonderful memories, and hundreds of nights anchored in special remote coves and harbors and quaint little towns. Jumping, diving, swimming, snorkeling, and lunches in Oyster Bay and Lake Michigan were enjoyed with our grandchildren, Julia, Jon Andrew, Jenica, Clarke, Claire, Jenevieve, Charles Jon, and Jaydee. Watching them grow and mature from toddlers to adults from the decks of our boats gave us hundreds of hours of family fun.

Special memories of mine were motoring fifteen miles down Lake Charlevoix to see the Boyne City Fourth of July fireworks and returning in darkness and, if lucky, in the glow of the moon and its reflection on the water. We passed the lights and outlines of small cottages and large seasonal homes along the lake's shoreline while everyone was tasked to watch for crowded boat traffic and to be the first to see the Coast Guard tower lights and entrance into Round Lake and home. A pilgrimage of sorts.

Skiing in Vail: Jon C., Jon, Joan, Jessica, Jenifer, Carol.

THE NINETIES

TRIVIAL PURSUITS AND TRAVEL

AT THE BEGINNING OF THE LAST DECADE OF THE MILLENNIUM, the United States population was now over 250 million and a new 1990 Fleetwood Cadillac would cost $32,500 and $20 to fill the tank. A gallon of whole milk was only $1.10. American politics was relatively calm, and the internet was gaining ground as the new form of social communications that would forever change the world. The public gorged itself on super-size hamburgers, French fries, and 7-Eleven big gulp sodas. Microsoft helped Apple avoid bankruptcy with a $150 million investment. On April 24, 1990, NASA's space shuttle *Discovery* launched the Hubble Space Telescope, rewriting the complexities and expansiveness of man's understanding of the universe. My generation was the first to have a scientific explanation of how it began and how it works. Astrophysicists came to realize that the universe was a lot bigger and a lot stranger than we imagined. In 1993 astronaut Story Musgrave and his team were launched into space to chase down, rescue, and repair the faulty Hubble Space Telescope. The operation involved one of the most challenging spacewalks in NASA's history. Five missions in eleven days for a total of over 35 hours, 370 miles above Earth moving over 17,000 miles an hour. Musgrave said of his experience with Hubble, "It bridges a gap between cosmology, theology, philosophy, and astronomy. It tends to shed a light on who we are. And who humanity is." Bravery lives amongst us. Another space hero.

A grandchild once asked me, "Do you believe in miracles?" "Of course I do, I said. Just look in the mirror, what you see is a miracle. Listen to the thunder, smell the rain, gaze into a clear night sky, and try to count the stars. Embrace the cold wind and snow of a mountain, taste the salt of a warm ocean and it's sting in your eyes. Fall in love. Yes, I believe in miracles."

Later in this decade at California's Stanford University, two guys named Page and Brin were in their dormitory creating a new online search technology that became known as Google—an odd name that opened the world's accumulated knowledge at the tip of one's forefinger. A quarter of a century later, humanity is still struggling with the consequences of such a terrific change. The technological revolution has no end. AI is next.

* * *

And back home in our little village of Charlevoix, my friend and occasional business partner, Rik Lobenherz, put together nine Charlevoix investors (Carol and I at 7%) to purchase acreage on the northeast side of town off US 31 to build and operate what would be known as the Charlevoix Country Club. A few of my co- founders and their wives became lifelong friends including Don and Ellen Jesmore, John and Zita Winn, Charlie and Janna Winn, and Arch and Trish Wright. Trish was a good friend of mine from early Edgewater Inn days. She was a copy editor and taught technical writing at North Central Michigan College. I called her after I finished my first draft. I told her about "Who's To Know," and that I was filled with doubt and fear. She read my story and gave me the support and timely boost of confidence.

"Jon, you can do this. You are a good writer. Keep at it. You need to keep going and finish it." Thank you Trish.

The Country Club was a big deal socially for a number of local and seasonal residents. Membership and real estate sales grew and became a large part of our family's social circle, and we were glad to be an integral part of it. Unfortunately, as the operations grew, so did the operational overhead that gave way to friction among some founders. The stress of hiring and firing chefs, golf pros, and meeting payroll became a problem. After several years the founders unanimously decided to sell the golf/restaurant club side of the business, at a loss, and to keep the real estate development property. The club was not a good investment but lots of fun for a few good years.

We had sold our home at 5 Thistle Downs for $675,000 and from June to September we stayed in Unit 120 with the girls at Edgewater Inn and *Engenuity*. In the fall, we rented a house on McSauba Road for the winter while we built our next home at 217 1/2 Park Avenue overlooking the Pine River Channel and Lake Michigan. I named it Stonecliff.

Stonecliff

After finishing the Edgewater Inn, it became increasingly difficult to put a significant project of meaningful size together. Several attempts were explored. During this time, I entered into an option to purchase a struggling condominium development on Mackinac Island. It was coincidentally called Stone Cliff and consisted of some six-plex condominiums and an event building with acreage to expand. Unfortunately, the seller could not fulfill the usual conditions of the buy-sell agreement. I was really enthused to be involved in and working on Mackinac Island, so it was a frustrating disappointment.

Dick Georgi, a friend and Country Club co-founder, his brother, John Georgi from Florida, and Arch Wright invited me to be a part of a development company they were forming that would build a hotel condominium in St. Thomas, US Virgin Islands. It was located in an area called Crown Bay, an area I was familiar with. John Georgi had already made preliminary contacts when I flew to St. Thomas and met with the principals and some local government officials to check it out. Fun but another no go. I put time and effort into researching many real estate deals such as Pontchartrain Point, an old, platted site in St. Martin Bay on Lake Huron a few miles north of Mackinac Island, a hotel condominium in Beaver Creek, Colorado, and several others. At least I tried. I developed a small site condominium on US 31 about two miles west of Petoskey on Little Traverse Bay. We divided it into eight condominium residential site lots plus commercial acreage on the highway and called it Arrowhead Shores. I joined Rik and Arch Wright to buy and sell acreage parcels in Canada and a residential lot development above Young State Park on Boyne City Road in Boyne City called Timber Ridge.

I can remember a meeting with Jack Begrow during a working lunch at the Weathervane Restaurant. I gave him an $8^1/_2 \times 14"$ city site map and legal description with a diagram and measurements of our new home's lot, a block from downtown Charlevoix. We talked a little about the angles of the property, the side yard set-backs and my desire to have three stone fireplaces, and a 44-foot lap swimming pool with an integrated stone-faced waterfall in the lower level. All the time we were talking and occasionally eating our lunch, he was drawing or writing with a black sharpie on several paper napkins. He kept asking the waitress to bring more. Jack called me late that afternoon and told me to come to his office where he showed me four or five sketches of our new home. After we discussed the plan, which I thought was amazing, he gave me a bill for eight hours work. I said, "Jack, we just had lunch four hours ago, and you are charging me for eight hours. What's up with that?" Jack smiled his big grin, showing off the gap between his front teeth and said, "Anybody else would have taken two or three days, Jon." We both laughed. It was worth every penny. I traded some of his work for time in our Colorado ski condominium.

In the early spring of 1991, we started construction on our Park Avenue home. It proved to be my favorite house. I was at the site nearly every day, hands on, answering questions, incorporating unique ideas and interesting personal touches. I made a large plaster rendering of a beech tree on the entrance foyer wall that included imprints of leaves Carol gathered from a side yard tree that integrated an arched stained-glass window over the front door. I placed intermittent stone ledges on interior walls. It drove the drywallers crazy. We placed a big heavy "lucky stone" on the roof to the puzzlement of anybody who saw it. At the end of the first-floor bedroom hallway, I made a full-size paper pattern of small irregular sized pieces of mirror that Mike's Glass cut and helped install. It was the first, and in all likelihood, the last time they were asked to take a perfect 3' x 8' mirror and make it look like a broken puzzle. I loved it. We placed a large and very heavy rock of several tons in the lower level and built the stairway system around and above it. I used to tell visitors that it was found in its place and was too heavy to move. I also placed an odd-colored stone on the floor between the swimming pool and sliding glass doorway and told guests that it was a meteor.

Ironically, Stonecliff was built on a sand dune and no stones bigger than a baby's little finger were ever found on the site. Every stone that was and was not seen was purchased and delivered from a quarry in Rogers City in the making of Stonecliff. It was our home for nearly ten years and is the only home we regretted selling.

Later that summer we entered *Engenuity* in the Venetian's evening lighted boat parade and won first prize—two for two— and the next day departed Charlevoix for our annual trip to the North Channel. In a few days we were settled in the small cove at Croker Island, one of our favorite anchorages. Sometimes after dinner and the day's wind had settled into a soft summer breeze, I would climb a short overgrown, rocky trail to the top of the island and sit on a smooth remnant of the 500-million-year-old Laurentian Mountains. It overlooked the waters of the North Channel, other islands, and indiscriminate rock outcroppings. The moment always reassured me that the cycle of life is a perpetual ending. A never-ending end. Just like the fate of an Indian or a French fur trader or a long-gone yachtsman, and everyone before me who was lucky enough to have sat in this very place to wonder. Everyone and everything ends. We are here for a mere infinitesimal fraction of time and very soon the world will never notice our absence.

Dreadful as the thought implies, it actually would envelope me with a sense of gratitude and contentment.

Contentment is the key to happiness. To be content is the key. —JAH

During the winter of 1992–93, I built a hydroplane boat from a kit that came in a heavy, big, six-ft-long flat cardboard box from upstate New York. I cleared an area in our garage at Stonecliff and kept it about 55 degrees with the help of an electric space heater. We named it *Goofy* after a Disney cartoon character. It was only used a few times before it was put to rest for several years in our boat barn, before being launched at the cottage's community beach for Carol's and my 50th wedding anniversary. It was a wicked blast, to be going 20 miles an hour when the brain is thinking 100. The last and best of my boat building memories.

* * *

February 3, 1992, was a momentous date in our family's history. Julia Grace Hisey entered the world as our first grandchild. Later that month I attended 40 hours of classroom work as a student with the Holloway Real Estate Institute in Petoskey, and after a state test in Traverse City, I became a licensed real estate agent in the State of Michigan. Also, Rik Lobenherz (15%) and I formed Iroquois Point Development. It consisted of 22 platted lots in the Upper Peninsula on the beautiful shores of Lake Superior near Brimley, Michigan. All of the lots sold within a few years.

1992, Venetian First Place.

During Charlevoix's 1992 Venetian Festival we once again entered *Engenuity* in the evening's lighted boat parade. We put Joan on skis in a two-piece bikini on the windshield facing toward the bow and over 15 family and a few guests were on board to cheer her on. Our boat's theme was "Summer of 92 … NOT." It was a cold summer. Awarded first place; three for three.

During my fifties my second and thankfully last mid-life crisis sneaked in before I knew it. Accompanied occasionally with bouts of mild clinical depression. Melancholy can be confusing or just annoying. Depression can be menacing or even dangerous. It led to excessive drinking, confusion, and conflicts within my family and business. The fence was broken, causing some reputational damage and embarrassment. Fortunately, the complexities of depression eventually peeled away and left the way it came. Quietly.

* * *

In June, Jack Begrow introduced me to the Kirchers of Boyne Country. They had become the largest privately owned ski company in the United States and were looking to partner with an outside builder/developer to design and manage construction of a duplex style single family project in Boyne Highlands, Harbor Springs. It was to be developed alongside their famous Heather golf course. Ironically, it was located near the base of the ski run where I had wiped out the beginner ski class a few years earlier. In short order, after an initial meeting with Everett Kircher, his son Stephen, and a few Boyne managers and a follow-up lunch, we worked out an agreement where I was to pay them $25,000 per unit when sold. Boyne provided all the condominium attorney fees from Bill Meyers of Dykema Gossett, the water and sewer, and all underground utilities including the road construction and paving. They gave me total control on my side of the agreement.

I hired Bill Johnson's firm to create the site plan and Jack completed all the construction drawings. I can vividly remember walking through the woods just a few yards in front of an 8-ft-wide bladed bulldozer, holding a copy of the site plan, and occasionally stopping to wrap and tie red plastic tape around trees that I wanted saved as we carved out the new roadway between two Heather fairways. I named the project Greystone.

After completing fourteen units, I decided to move on. The Kirchers continued the project with a in-house project manager. They were very accommodating and good people to work with. On reflection, it continues to amaze me how I was able to enter this multimillion-dollar partnership with very little of my own money. I am sure Everett Kircher did a complete background check on me because his right-hand man Art Tebow was a former FBI guy.

*　*　*

On June 29, 1993, our first grandson was born and christened Jon Andrew Hisey. It was a beautiful early summer afternoon in Charlevoix on August 21, 1993, when I gave away our daughter Joan to Todd D. Stebbins. Joan meticulously choreographed her wedding like it was a broadway production. The evenings reception was at Staffords Petoskey Bayview Inn. I was able to surprise her when I changed the father daughter dance song to Whitney Houston's rendition of "I Will Always Love You." It wasn't very long before the dance floor cleared, leaving Joan and me crying together surrounded by family and guests. Matrimony can be tough on a father.

In 1994, I started Cottage Pointe Development, Inc., to develop a narrow lot line site condominium project and to build "cottage" type single family homes within the Charlevoix Country Club. Like Greystone, it was bordered along and between fairways of the golf course.

In May, as my 50th birthday approached, my natural tendencies of occasional melancholy, brooding, introspection, and thoughts of mortality morphed into an idea to spend a few days alone, and I made my feelings very clear to Carol and the children. I did not want under any circumstances a party of any kind, period. No friends, no singing, no laughing, no dancing, no acquaintances, no nothing, period. Just me, myself, and I.

So, I decided to go camping somewhere, anywhere in the Upper Peninsula. I bought a sleeping bag and a small tent and some basic beginner gear. I had very little experience camping and had never spent a solo night in the "wild." On the morning of May 18, I methodically organized and carefully packed Carol's black Chevy Blazer with everything one would need for a few days of solitude, kissed Carol and the girls goodbye, and wished Jessica a happy birthday. I told them not to worry and that I would return in a few days, as a changed new man. With a slight nervous smile, I waved goodbye.

No plans, just drove north across the "Mighty Mac" to the Upper Peninsula with a Michigan road map by my side. About 4:00 in the afternoon, after exploring several desolate two track roads for my first night of camp, I found myself somewhere close to Trout Lake. Anxiety started to creep in. Realizing I was less than an hour's drive to our Iroquois Pointe development on the shores of Lake Superior, a plan soon materialized, and I headed north. Luckily, no one had started to build on any of the sold lots. I turned off the road and drove down a pathway toward the lake and, as security, dragged a nearby dead tree behind me across the trail.

Dusk had quickened its pace by the time my campsite was set up and my small Indian fire was ready to cook my can of baked beans, a sliced potato and a cheap steak. It wasn't long before I proceeded to enjoy my almost warm beans, with a half-cooked potato and pieces of chewy steak with a tepid can of beer and two small airline bottles of bourbon with my new friend Jim Beam.

I was feeling pretty good about myself at 50.

After tending the fire down to a few embers, I crawled into my tent and wrangled myself into my new sleeping bag for the night. Sometime during the night, I awoke from a timid sleep, eyes opened wide and ears perked to strange noises of the dark. I never could have imagined how many unknown weird sounds there are in the woods after the lights go out. I can still remember hearing footsteps from the broken twigs and rustled leaves and men's voices from the woods, "Here he is, over there. Over here guys!" and more. I laid there, fraught with fear, straining slow breaths being still and quiet, expecting doom at any moment before eventually giving way to a whiskey sleep.

At first light I peeked out of my tent to survey my environment, walked down to the lake and splashed my face with the clear, cold Superior. I broke camp, haphazardly threw everything into the back of the Blazer, hauled the dead tree away, still in its place, to the side of the trail and arrived home before lunch, hugging and kissing my family. *A changed man.*

Relieved to be home after my 50th, even though a little earlier than expected, I was nevertheless glad I dodged any birthday party or fuss that the 50-year milestone sometime brings. Jessica and I celebrated that night with Carol and Jenifer with candles, leftover cake, and the remains of yesterday's ice cream.

On May 28, a beautiful blue sky, northern Michigan spring day, Tracy and Chris Sell had invited Carol and me to a 5:00 p.m. automobile scavenger hunt at the Ferry Beach Pavilion on Lake Charlevoix. I was usually a little shy in crowds and never good at small talk. Reluctantly Carol convinced me that we had to go because Tracy and Chris were good friends. She said, "I'm sure it will be a small gathering with beer and hot dogs. We should be home early."

We arrived a little after 5:00 to a rather large crowd. "Wow. There is a lot of people here," I mentioned to Carol. "Yes, there is," she said, as I gave her a quizzical look. SURPRISE!!!!!! Dumbfounded I said, "What surprise?" as a big "Happy Birthday Jon" sign appeared! My jaw dropped and my face turned red as I reached for something to hang on to when Tracy handed me a cold can of beer. Then I saw my mother, dad, Darleen, and all my children come out of nowhere to join in the surprise. Many friends, and friends I didn't even know were friends, were there, all wearing white T-shirts with a large image of my 5th grade school picture imprinted on the front. I was shocked. Shocked beyond belief. Surprised beyond surprise. The scavenger hunt proceeded with several teams, each having clues, all pertaining to what they perceived to be my personal unusual idiosyncrasies. Each team had a single-use camera to verify the completed tasks. As groups finished, they made their way to Edgewater's conference room where Joan and Jon collected the cameras and rushed to Merrill's camera shop (she had stayed open to develop the pictures for us). Each of the team's photos were then placed on large foam boards with easels.

To summarize: some of the photos included teams in the Charlevoix city jail, interrupting Saturday's Catholic Mass, some perhaps confessed to the priest before next Saturday's mass, and a Hell's Angels motorcycle club gathering in Ironton. One team wrapped my old beat-up pickup truck with two rolls of duct tape and there was a photo of Tracy sitting on my toilet at Stonecliff using my private phone. One photograph showed someone reaching into a trash can to get a day-old donut with a bite out of it. I always bought day-old donuts when I could. How did they know that? And many more.

The night ended with Jessica by my side and jokes and toasts with me as the punch line and a dinner catered by our own Edgewater Cafe. One story that I think warrants repeating and that I remembered after all these years is when Ted McGlinch stood up near the end of the evening and said this, "I have a little story about Jon that you might like".

"Three men went up to the pearly gates to heaven. St. Peter came to the door and said to the first guy, why are you here? Well, I was in a terrible car accident, and I got thrown onto the highway and skidded down the road about a hundred yards. It almost took every piece of skin off my body. I laid in the hospital for several weeks. It was very painful, and I finally succumbed to my injuries, and I'd like to know if I can come in through the gate. St. Pete looked at him and said, you cannot come in. You have not suffered enough. He turned to the next guy and asked him what can I do for you? Well, I had a beautiful home and one day it caught on fire. My family was inside the house, and I kept going back in and finally rescued them and my family dog. I got second and third degree burns all over my body. I laid in the hospital for over three months and finally succumbed from my painful injuries. I'd like to come in through the gates and into heaven. St. Pete took one look at him and said, sir you have not suffered enough. You must go back.

"St. Peter looked at the third guy and asked, what are you here for? And the third man said, I was peeling potatoes one evening for my wife while sitting at the kitchen table. I got a little cut on my finger, and we could not find a bandaid, and was afraid of getting an infection. So, I called my neighbor Jon Hisey and he came over with one. St. Pete interrupted his spiel, wait a minute, wait just a minute. You know Jon Hisey? Well, sure I do, he's my neighbor. St. Pete said to the third man, You know Jon Hisey? Come on in my friend. You have suffered enough."

Actually, this birthday party was a much more memorable, positive, exciting day than the May 18 solitary event. I loved every minute of it. Thank you, family.

*   *   *

On May 27, 1995, we were blessed with our third grandchild Jenica Rose Hisey. That summer we departed for our annual trip to the North Channel, with the usual stops including Government Island, Detour Village, Meldrum Bay, the North and South Benjamin Islands, Croker Island, Little Current, Covered Portage Cove, and Killarney. Bill and Jeanne Martin joined us with their boat along with Rik and Kathryn's and another boat with four of Bill's friends. On our first night we anchored together in Government Bay located within the Les Cheneaux Islands in northern Lake Huron. I had alerted my friends Bill and Pat Sherman from Charlevoix that we may anchor there.

Shortly after we all got situated, along came Bill Sherman in his Zodiac dinghy to greet us. He looked surprised to see four boats and the number of people I was boating with, but nevertheless, he graciously invited all of us to cocktails and dinner at his summer home on a nearby island. Everybody loaded up on *Engenuity* and followed Bill just a couple miles before tying up at the tee end of his dock. The Shermans were amazing hosts. They fed us, entertained us, and provided everyone with plenty of beverages and lots of laughter all around. At the evening's end while heading back to the dock, Carol said, "Wait a minute; we should get a picture of everybody." So, the twelve of us stopped at the end of the dock in front of *Engenuity*, posing for Carol to take our picture. Suddenly a loud crash and screaming erupted as the dock collapsed; luckily no one was hurt, just some wet feet and legs and a few bottoms. Eventually we all managed to climb our way onboard and as we were pulling away, we could see by moonlight the lingering shock on their faces as our generous hosts made an effort to smile awkwardly while waving us goodbye, or was it a wave of good riddance?

After a week of cruising with friends, Carol and I stayed in the North Channel a few days longer and returned to one of our favorite anchorages in the small bay at Croker Island on our way home to Charlevoix. As we were leaving, Carol took the helm while I was stowing lines and getting gear shipshape as we slowly entered the narrow channel that guided us toward Robertson Light at the north end of Clapperton Island.

I took the wheel from Carol and did a quick 360 look around to make sure all was clear before giving the engines FULL throttle. Instantly, BAM! Full stop. It sounded like an explosion as *Engenuity* lurched up onto rocks and boulders. We stopped dead in our tracks. I could not believe it; we had been in these waters several times, even escorting newbies on how to get through the hazards to reach the Benjamin and Croker Islands.

Here we were. Stuck. I immediately put on my fins, mask, and snorkel to explore the depths and check the damage while Carol grabbed her purse, ready to jump into the dinghy, if necessary. I stepped off the swim ladder into water that was barely up to my knees. I got right back up on the boat, tore off my gear, and examined the storage compartment under the floor in the main salon which had already accumulated a few inches of water. "Carol, calm down! The last thing this boat is going to do is sink."

I then radioed the Canadian Coast Guard and gave them my position and condition of the boat, and that we were in no danger of sinking. While talking to them another Coast Guard person cut in saying, "Are you the boat grounded on the Pigs and Sows?" I said, "Yes, we are. Well, I am at Robertson's light and I can see you. You are way west of the channel. "Duh." It was about that time I noticed Jack and Barb Begrow motoring by on their sailboat *Mint Julep* a few hundred yards to our east in the channel where we should have been. I was so embarrassed, I told Carol to duck. We didn't even know they were in the area. The Coast Guard boat came up in a few minutes and threw us a couple of heavy tow lines and eventually, after several attempts, we finally managed to slide backwards into deeper water to the sounds of excruciating painful noises of the hull's bottom scraping against the rocks. We had one good engine and propeller on the starboard side and after discussing the situation with the Coast Guard, we all decided it would be best to slowly limp our way 20 miles back to Little Current. We would communicate by marine radio every 10 or 15 minutes to monitor our progress. Between Carol manually bailing out the salon storage compartment and the automatic bilge pumps, we were able to keep up with the leaks.

On the way back to Little Current I radioed Boyle Marine and made arrangements to haul out *Engenuity* and hopefully make the necessary repairs. We spent the night on our boat which was now high and dry on large wood blocks in the marina's yard. My mother was in Charlevoix with the children, and they arrived the next day to pick us up. After about six or seven weeks and over $10,000 of repair costs, and a free souvenir coffee mug, Carol and I along with brother Jim and nephew Chris, who drove from their home in Connecticut, picked up the boat and safely returned her to Charlevoix.

Somebody, we never knew for sure, put a display ad in the *Charlevoix Courier* newspaper with a photo of me and a big caption that said, "Jon Hisey Captain of the Year Pigs and Sows."

* * *

In October 1995 Carol and I flew to Paris, France, and spent our days touring the city. We then rented a car for a week and proceeded to get "stuck" on the Arc de Triomphe's hideous multiple unmarked lanes on the roundabout. After several trips around and around and hollering between ourselves and fellow motorists, I stopped the car. Carol got out and waved some magic to the honking and screeching of the motoring chaos while guiding us to an exit. We drove through the countryside toward Normandy and its World War II infamous beaches and the immaculate sobering and somber American Cemetery and Memorial. Another one of our memorable stops on this trip was at Mount St. Michele, a famous 1,500-year-old monastery island of barren rock that is located on the shores of the English Channel. We stayed at the Hotel Mt Blanc, in a cheap room (as usual) in a great location. Room 305 was three flights up a creaking, narrow, winding stairway with a small view to the sea and mainland. We parked the car as directed near the island just off the roadway. In the morning, we looked out the window to see that the car park area and causeway to the mainland was covered with several inches of water and had to wait a few hours for the tide to subside before continuing our road trip.

On the return drive to Paris, we spent a night in Rouen, Normandy's capital nestled along the Seine River about a hundred miles northwest of Paris. We stopped for dinner at the oldest restaurant in France (how could we not stop). "La Couronne" was established in 1345, 150 years before Columbus crossed the Atlantic Ocean. It was located directly across the street from the very spot 19-year-old Joan of Arc was burned at the stake. Soon after we were seated next to a window with a streetscape view, I asked the maître d' some historical questions about the building. Soon Carol and I were following our new friend throughout the ancient building, as he pointed out centuries-old names and dates carved into large heavy timbers. Downstairs, upstairs, and into tiny rooms with nooks and crannies and secret doors. What a treat. It pays to be nice and to show sincere interest, respect, and curiosity to a stranger's place in the world, (it's also nice when they can speak a little English). I sometimes think that I would have been a good history teacher. France was another all-around delight.

* * *

Clarke Daniel Stebbins was born February 27, 1996, and spent one week in the hospital before going home to Joan and Todd. After visiting little Clarke at the hospital, Carol and I departed for Abaco Island in the Bahamas to stay with Don and Ellen Jesmore at their winter home for several days along with Rik and Kathryn.

* * *

The unique reason for including our 1997 North Channel cruise was when we rendezvoused with Jack Begrow and friends on his sailboat. We anchored together in "The Pool" at the end of the Baie of Finn, a regular stop of ours. We walked a rugged two-mile trail up to Lake Topaz, (our first time) a very deep glacier formed lake. We jumped from the cliffs and dove from the shore into the crystal clear cold dark blue water. Lake Topaz became a must-do stop every time we were close to the Baie of Finn. My chapel. The ultimate favorite of my favorites.

In the spring of 1998, while skiing in Park City with family, an out-of-control beginner skier hit Carol near the bottom of the Monitor slope. His ski tip cut through her ski pants and lodged just below the knee. She weened herself off crutches after six painful weeks. I learned how to operate the dishwasher, do the laundry, and boil an egg.

We closed the decade by purchasing a two-bedroom plus den, two-bath Windward Condominium (unit 122) along the par 3 number 4 fairway in Windstar Country Club, Naples, Florida. It included a golf membership.

Following is a frequently told anecdote as to how we ended up in Naples. When we opened the new clubhouse at the Charlevoix Country Club, the founders invited a large gathering of new and potential members to an early evening open house party. Anytime you want a big turnout, just give them free food and drinks. Our tasks were to meet and greet our guests and, hopefully, entice a few to become members of our new club. I was standing with my son Jon among several guests wearing their penny loafers without pennies and without socks and pastel v-neck cashmere sweaters draped and tied over their shoulders with ironed khaki shorts and braided nautical waist belts. Out of my league. Over my head. We were trying to "sell" the benefits of the Club. I must admit that I may have been a little "full of it" and totally out of my self-effac-ing natural character, when I began to tell my audience that Carol and I had just purchased a second home at a golf club in Naples. We were looking forward to golf year-round and making new friends in our seasonal club, when one of the guests interrupted my spiel and asked, "Say Jon, how did you end up in Naples?" "Well … Carol and I decided to fly into Tampa and rent a car to drive south to look for a winter getaway that had a golf amen-ity. We stopped intermittently to explore potential golf course projects that were within a few minutes of the I-75 corridor." I started to explain in various details where we stopped in towns like Clearwater, Bradenton, Sarasota, Venice, and others that eventually led us to our country club in high-end Naples. Digging myself into a hole of awkward convoluted embarrassment, before I could finish my next braggadocious sentence, son Jon thankfully cut me off, and in a distinct clear and rather loud voice said, "Well I know how Dad ended up in Naples!" All attention turned to my son. "They were driving south on

Jon and Carol at the Country Club around 1997.

I-75 and saw a big green and white highway sign. LAST EXIT BEFORE TOLL." From time to time someone will still stop and ask with a teasing grin, "Hey Jon how did you end up in Naples?" Occasionally through my years, a timely good jab was necessary to set me straight, but this one is the one I remember.

*　*　*

We entered *Engenuity* a third time for the Venetian Boat Parade with a boat full of family and friends. Mom volunteered to be towed behind the boat in our small rubber dinghy with a sign and a spotlight focused on her. Then the generator broke. No prize. After Venetian we spent another two weeks in the North Channel. You may be tired of the North Channel routine, but for me, it was one of my favorite places in the world. I am eternally grateful for each cruise north that became an adventure of spectacular beauty and unique experiences. Frankly, I miss it terribly.

*　*　*

In the fall of 1998 Cathay Pacific Airlines was offering a 30-day round-trip ticket from Los Angeles to Asia for only $999 that included up to 17 transfer flights. We flew on November 3rd to Los Angeles for the night and the next afternoon we were waiting in the ticket line with excitement and anxiety for our first 16-hour nonstop transpacific flight to Hong Kong. I happened to be wearing a white button-down shirt and a new black crewneck sweater. With a smile I handed the young Asian ticket agent our passports and flight information envelope. She returned the smile and said, "Good afternoon, Father." I quickly deduced the innocent misunderstanding and responded, "Thank you my dear." In a few minutes she handed me our tickets with another friendly smile saying, "Have a nice flight Father," and as I began to turn away, I said, "God bless you child." I just couldn't resist. Sitting at the departure gate I opened the ticket jacket. Front row, first class. We could not believe it, thank you Jesus!

We spent the next 30 days traveling, each with just a small carry-on piece of luggage plus Carol's big purse. During a few days of sightseeing in Hong Kong, we were able to locate the tiny upstairs windowless room where Jenifer stayed while traveling home from teaching English in South Korea a few years earlier. From Hong Kong we flew to Cebu and Manila in the Philippines; General MacArthur's Corregidor Island, Sri Lanka; Bangkok, Thailand; Singapore; and Bali.

Sri Lanka is a small island nation, and often rated as one of the world's most beautiful islands. It's population mostly practiced Buddhism. At the time we visited it was still plagued by a civil war. Fighting was contained in the northern section of the island. Our first night was in Columbo, where there were machine gun nests throughout the city. The US currency was king to the rupee dollar that provided a huge exchange rate. We hired a driver to take us to the seaside resort town of Gallee for a two-night stay.

From there we then took a six-hour third class train ride to Kandy near the center of the island. We have been on dozens of trains in our travels, but this one was by far, remembered the most for its deplorable condition from filth and age. The passengers were poor, I'd say some of the poorest we've ever seen. So very sad, and troubling; motionless mothers with babies, cripples without crutches, and beggars for just a snack or a coin. They were stuck by just breathing. Clothes were worn thin and dirty, rags just draped around skeletons. Their suffering was mentally exhausting. We seemed helpless. Why are they here? Why are we here? Buddhists are waiting to die to be reborn into a better life. I hope they make it. Christians are waiting to die to go to their heaven. As I grow older, my view or opinion of spirituality has taken a circuitous route from agnostic to born again Christian, to God help me. I just can't or won't lockstep with organized religion. I'll risk my soul to deism and the origins of life. My only prayer now is; "I pray there is no hell".

The train station wasn't much better. I was shocked when I walked into the bathroom to pee. The place was packed with men against a long urinal waiting for a spot. The entire floor was flooded with about 1/2 inch of pee and a little poop. The stench was unbearable beyond breathable. I stepped outside and found a nearby bush circled by men. In front of the train station there were several cars with drivers waiting for hire. We picked the driver with the biggest smile and cleanest car. What luck. He gave us an in-depth tour of the city and dropped us off at a hotel he recommended and told us to be ready at 9:00 a.m. for pick up the next day. He drove us and tutored us and waited while we explored the parks, temples, wildlife reserves and mountains and back to the coast that evening to a hotel near the airport. While checking into the hotel I overheard three men discussing the next early mornings drive to the airport. I realized that we were on the same flight. Frankly they looked like gangsters of the mob. Dressed in dark shiny suits and shiny black shoes and combed back shiny black hair. I whispered to Carol, "I'm going to see if we can hitch a ride to the airport."

"No Jon, please Jon no. They look like killers. Please no." They asked about luggage, and I showed them our carry-ons. They huddled a few minutes and said, "Meet us right here at 3:00 a.m. sharp. Don't be late. We will leave without you." Carol didn't sleep at all that night. An oversized black Mercedes showed up at 3:05 in the morning. Carol and I did not say a word during the 30-minute ride to the airport, each of us hoping that we were going to the airport and not a hole in the ground.

At the airport we were stopped at the entrance gate and had to get out and be searched while other soldiers checked the car for guns and explosives. The planes pilots kept the cabin lights down and all of the window shades were kept closed. We were guided to our seats with the help of the crew's small flashlights. Even the planes exterior lights were kept off. During takeoff the plane accelerated so fast it seemed like we were going straight up. During the flight I was told that all international flights were early and kept dark because the rebel separatists were threatening sabotage.

In Bali I hired a dive outfit with another guy who was Canadian and worked for Nike in the Philippines. We drove over 70 kilometers one way on the most beautiful scenic two-lane road I have ever been on. Our destination was a remote beach on the shores of the Indian Ocean. Children were there to help unload our gear and sell snacks and beer from a cooler. Our wetsuits were torn and frayed, and the scuba tanks and regulators looked like antiques. The driver turned out to be our dive master. He asked us some of the basic questions while we were wading into the ocean. Within a few minutes my new friend and I were struggling to keep up with our guide as we swam to the bottom. It was a serious dive into the open rusting hull of a World War II shipwreck in about 100 feet of water. Our decompression safety stops on our way up to the surface were half the recommended times, as our guide left us after only one. It was a little challenging and a nerve-racking dive, but beautiful and interesting. We both had a cold beach beer from a vendor's cooler and toasted our survival.

On the morning of November 22, we were in the City of Manila, Philippines. We packed our gear and with our well-worn guidebook took a cab to the bus station for a two-hour express bus ride to the remote village of Pagsanjan and the Magdapio River. Its claim to fame is the beautiful canoe ride upriver to the infamous last scene in Francis Ford Coppola's award-winning Vietnam War movie *Apocalypse Now*. It's where insane renegade Colonel Kurtz (Marlon Brando) was hiding with his men in a grotto compound and famously whispered his last words, "the horror … the horror."

We rented a small room across the street from the river and stowed our gear. We helped each other down some broken concrete stairs that stopped at the water's edge where a few canoes with lingering men were selling river tours. The river was beautiful in every way, a step back in time; natives in huts with white laundry hanging from a wire between trees, and a cow and chickens and goats grazing the greens along the river's edge. We were the only canoe on the river; it had a small, long-shaft outboard motor to ease travel upstream against the current. Two innocent white tourists with two natives, two machetes, and two paddles and a half tank of gas. The farther we went upstream, the shores of the jungles seemed to close in around us as we slowly advanced against the twists and the rapids growing more remote with each mile. Our worrisome fears were evident just by the look on our faces. What's worse was that we left our luggage with some money at the side of a small wood desk in the office of a rundown four-unit motel.

After finally reaching the grotto and tying up to a broken makeshift dock, we made a quick look around the grotto and its illustrious movie scene and returned to the canoe. The canoe chief, in broken English, pointed upriver and said, "Falls, going to falls." I replied with a strong no question needed voice, "No! No!" while pointing downriver and back to town. The driver pointed again upriver, "We go to pretty falls, to pretty falls we go," I kept my outstretched arm and pointed finger, "Go back. No falls. Go back to town now." It was a quiet ride back and when we said our goodbyes and *gracias* I gave them each ten dollars US cash, about equal to the whole cost of the adventure.

Carol decided that she did not, would not, spend the night there. We gathered our gear and told the room clerk to keep the small nightly fee that we had paid and asked about a bus back to Manila. She looked at the one-handed clock on the wall and said, "The last bus leaves in about twenty minutes. We fast walked to a nearby corner where I flagged down a young man riding a scooter and asked, "Can you take us to the bus stop?" He put our luggage on his floor and in a big basket up front. I jumped on behind him while Carol barely fit on the small space behind me squeezing so hard around my waist that I couldn't take a full breath until we got to the bus stop. The bus was loaded; some folks were standing. We were the only tourists and had to split up to find a place to sit, each putting our luggage on our laps. There were chickens and babies and friendly, happy folks with generous smiles, some with missing teeth. They were kind and accommodating and a few could speak only limited English. It was actually kind of fun. The bus was a "local," meaning it stopped very frequently on the over three-hour ride back to Manila. We were tired, hungry, and safe. I suppose we always were. The city was busy, dark, and damp with odors from the afternoon rain.

Carol and I walked past vendors and avoided sidewalk sleepers as we approached the same hotel where we started our 14-hour exciting day. I remembered thinking to myself how much I loved to travel.

* * *

Our beautiful fifth grandchild, Claire Joan Stebbins, was born on April 5, 1999. We closed out the century on December 30th by purchasing a new 39' Robertson and Caine catamaran sailboat from the Moorings in Road Town, Tortola, British Virgin Islands for $250,000 and put it into their rental fleet. I christened the boat *Resolution*. Carol and I enjoyed many memorable sailing weeks throughout the British Virgin Islands with some family and guests. But, not as many as predicted or hoped for, and sold *Resolution* in 2005, at a loss. I made a resolution then to never make another large boat investment again. Never ever again.

Resolution

Ever never. An ironclad resolution.

We spent the new millennium eve at a large party in the Charlevoix Country Club, complete with black tuxedos and ladies in floor-length gowns. A special date to be sure and a witness to a new century and a thousand-year anniversary, only the second time in modern history. Unforgettable, a witness to a fateful turn of humanities calendar.

THE 2000s

DAYS OF CHANGE
AND A LOT MORE TRAVEL

THE FIRST DECADE OF THE NEW CENTURY started with a contested presidential election that eventually was decided, for the first time in US history, by our Supreme Court and by Vice President Al Gore who graciously accepted and then conceded his loss to George W. Bush. Saving the country from dangerous uncertainty and confusion, a foreshadowing event. The stock market crashed twice within the decade, and Carol's new 2000 Chrysler convertible set us back $27,480. Home mortgage interest rates were a little over 8%. Everyone seemed to be wearing track suits, hoodies, and tennis shoes on airplanes and Sunday church and nice restaurants. The beleaguered gay population was finally getting the acceptance they deserved while opening closet doors around the world.

The year began with sadness within our family when on January 15, Darleen Hisey died suddenly with heart failure in Sweetwater, Tennessee, while traveling south with Dad to attend Mom's 80th birthday in Clearwater. I have fond memories of her. She played the role of stepmother with kindness and patience, as well as being a great cook.

My friend Tracy Sell formed a new corporation and asked me to help him purchase the Lodge Motel (adjacent to the north side of Edgewater Inn property) for $1.5 million with a large loan from Charlevoix State Bank. I used my credit worthiness at Northwestern Savings Bank and Trust for a 25% stake in the Lodge Development Co., as a "silent partner." The new company was obligated to pay my loan back, which it did. In preparation of Tracy's upcoming retirement after 18 years as owner of the Lodge and almost 40 years masterfully operating the Edgewater Inn Hotel, he sold The Lodge in 2018 to a downstate developer. The new owner invested several million dollars into the property and renamed it "The Earl" after Earl Young, the original builder of the Lodge in the mid 1950s.

In May we started our first week of sailing adventures on our new 39' catamaran sailboat, *Resolution.* Over the next four years we were lucky to have cruised with over 100 days in and around the beautiful British Virgin Islands. We also sailed on sister ships in the Sea of Cortez, Mexico, and the Lesser Antilles Island of St. Martin in the northeastern Caribbean Sea. Another foolish investment, but if you want my advice—do it! Never say never.

In the spring, I enrolled in a 40-hour sea captain's class in Clearwater while staying at my mother's condominium, followed by a three-hour final exam in Cape Coral, Florida (my first time in the Cape). I became a licensed Captain of the United States Coast Guard as a Merchant Marine Officer that allowed me to take six paying customers up to 50 miles offshore.

*   *   *

Grandpa and Julia on *Goofy* in Lake Charlevoix.

After a few years of spending a few months each winter in our Naples Condominium, we decided to purchase a single-family home on a canal with Gulf of Mexico access. Unfortunately, we soon realized that the Naples area property values had escalated beyond our financial comfort level.

Charlie and Janna Winn invited us to their Cape Coral home and graciously escorted us to various properties with their real estate agent as a guide. By the afternoon of the third day everyone was pretty well exhausted from looking through kitchens, closets, and neglected bathrooms. Nothing seemed to fit or grab us. We were tired and disappointed and had packed our suitcases when the agent called Charlie about a house that wasn't very far from the Winns. She had heard that this house had a pending offer, but it was still in the area's multi list. It was our last possibility to check out on our way back to Naples. We all toured the home at 5603 S.W. 11th Avenue, Cape Coral. We liked it. Charlie then took us on his boat to see the house from the canal's viewpoint, and within two hours we had an accepted offer. I flew back in early June and closed on our new house. It became the home that we have owned the longest and introduced us to our lasting neighborhood friendships with Ron and Beverly Taht, Mark Holman, Tom and Lynn Polacek, and Ron and Linda Stagliano, among others.

During our 2001 summer trip to the North Channel, our first grandchild, nine-year-old Julia Grace joined us. It was a real treat to finally spend some one-on-one time with her, to introduce her to the world of difference, the scope of natural beauty and nature and the fun and joy it provides. Later in the week daughter Jenifer and her friend Jen Frabis joined us in Little Current for a few days of cruising.

* * *

September 11, 2001, started as a beautiful late summer Tuesday morning when I was in a Charlevoix Country Club founders' board meeting upstairs in the Clubhouse conference room. We were discussing mundane figures of budgets and membership goals while I was thinking of that night's league golf game when our comptroller Gary Moore knocked on the door and walked in while opening it. "Guys, the country is under attack. A plane has crashed into New York's World Trade Center building." He walked over to the TV on the wall and turned it on as we watched and witnessed the world change. Shortly and silently, we gathered our belongings and went home to fixate on live TV for the rest of the day as the horrific historical drama of the new century unfolded.

American Airlines flight 11 from Boston crashed into the north tower of the Trade Center at 8:45 a.m. with 20,000 gallons of jet fuel that caused it's collapse to the street at 10:30 a.m. United Airlines flight 175 targeted the south tower at 9:05 a.m. and it too collapsed within the hour. American Airlines flight 77 departed Washington National Airport and circled over Washington D.C. before crashing into the west side of the Pentagon at 9:45 a.m. United flight 93 left from Newark, New Jersey, and was denied its target, assuming it was the Capitol, by several brave men and women who fought the hijackers and forced the plane to crash in a Pennsylvania field near Shanksville. A total of nearly 3000 innocent men, women, and children died that day.

On December 8, 1941, President Franklin D. Roosevelt declared that the Japanese sudden attack on Pearl Harbor on December 7 was a day that will live in infamy. I suggest that September 11, 2001, has become America's second day of infamy. Its repercussions changed the United States and the world in ways that we are still grappling with.

Near the end of Harbour Plaza's selling period there were three units remaining. A local businessman of questionable repute offered to buy all three condominiums that were in various stages of completion. I hesitated but accepted, and as a hedge I arranged a licensed realtor and mutual friend as a go-between who would benefit from a commission. This memory is not a good one and it pains me to include it within my life's story. Following is an ultra-condensed summary of events. Shortly after our closing on the three units, he started to ask unrealistic favors and exorbitant changes. He became belligerent, mean, and bullying. My so-called friend and go-between got up and went to the other side. My attorney became mute. I had no idea of how to handle it; my natural instincts and history of nonconfrontational successful negotiations failed me. He threatened me in person. He sued me for a huge amount of money for unfounded made-up scurrilous actions. I sued back and it dragged on for almost two years. I was a stranger to the language and protocols of the events. A "deer in headlights," as they say. We settled, no one won after many thousands of wasted dollars and attorney fees and time. We eventually sold the units. That's my brief recollection. You can't get his side of the story because within a year he was dead. He killed himself.

Again: It's not the contract you sign. It's the hand that you shake. I knew it. I ignored my own advice and paid with wasted worry.

On the eve of 2002, Mom made one of her usual trips to Charlevoix for the Christmas holidays with us and our growing family and celebrated a quiet New Year's Eve at a friend's house. The next morning Mom got up late and made an unusual complaint of not feeling well, that went unnoticed.

Soon after returning to Florida, she made an appointment with her doctor, who suggested she undergo testing for cancer, common for a colon cancer survivor of several years earlier. Carol and I had also returned to our place in Naples and decided to drive up to Clearwater to take Mom to her doctor's appointments and diagnostic tests. After the last round of exams, the doctor pulled me aside in the hospital's hallway and advised me that Mother had terminal pancreatic cancer. She recommended that arrangements be made for her children to be with her when she delivered the diagnosis to Mom.

Within 48 hours, brothers Jim, Jerry, Carol and I entered the small hospital room together. This is a clear unforgettable moment. When Mom looked up from her hospital bed and first saw her three boys together, she said, "Now I know I'm in trouble." After greetings and hugs, the doctor explained the disease and inevitable outcome. Six to twenty weeks. Mom said, "Now I am scared." She quickly, typically, accepted her fate. From that hospital room the doctor made arrangements to directly admit her to Sabal Palms Nursing Home in nearby Largo. Within the next few weeks all of her grandchildren visited to say their goodbyes. Joan and Jessica flew down for several days and Jenifer and Jon drove my new truck straight through from Charlevoix. Jenifer stayed the last few weeks to help. She spent a great amount of time alone with her grandmother, usually in the quiet evenings after dinner, maybe watching the small black and white TV or just whispering or listening to her grandmother sleep. Each treasuring these final moments in their own way.

She died Sunday morning on March 10, 2002, with Carol by her side and me running down the hallway, seconds later. I want to believe that she heard me say goodbye and that she was a good mom who was loved, and it was her time to fly—fly high. It was a bright light Florida morning while her lifeless body was being zipped up into a black plastic bag and lifted into the back of the waiting black hearse, as the surrounding Sunday church bells tolled, and I could hear the sound of the mourning doves, coo … coo … coo.

I've included the following anecdote because I think her request to hear it exemplifies her courage and attitude of acceptance of her fate, as she did throughout her life.

One special time I remember sitting with Mom, probably just reading a paper as she slept, when she opened her eyes and quietly said to me, "Jon, tell me the story again about the time you and the girls rented the horses." I answered, "The one in the Utah canyon with Jenifer and Jessica?" She whispered with a slight grin, "I think that's it."

A brief introduction leading up to the story would begin a few years earlier when Don Jesmore asked me to drive his 42' motor home from San Francisco to Charlevoix. Of course I said, "Yes. But I've never driven a motor home before. No problem, just avoid backing up and make wide turns." Typical Don. I piped up, "That's fantastic, I'll buy the gas." Don said, "Are you sure Jon? Ok." That was a mistake; six or seven mpg. Several weeks later, Don picked Carol and me up at the San Francisco airport with a rental car and took us to the nearby RV park. After a short explanation of the systems and review of handwritten reminder points, we drove Don and Ellen back to the airport hotel for their next morning flight home. We kept the rental car a few more days and toured the city and surroundings, which we loved, that included a drive over the famous Golden Gate Bridge.

We didn't have a due back date, so after a stop at Yosemite National Park we continued on to Las Vegas, Nevada, and camped for a night at the strip's only RV park. Not big gamblers, we each got a ten-dollar roll of quarters and decided to meet back in an hour at the resort's restaurant. Carol laughed when I showed her my unopened roll of quarters before she opened her small purse and pulled out her unopened roll of quarters. Gamblers we were not. We rendezvoused with Jessica and Jenifer, living in Park City at the time, at Utah's Zion National Park. We spent the day there, before driving to Bryce Canyon, and the girls spent another night with us in the motor home in the canyon's parking lot.

Now comes Mom's request: In the morning, we signed up for

an escorted horse ride into the canyon to see up close its famous, unique to the world, crimson red rock spires and hoodoos—unusual formations that took millions of years to evolve. In the corral the wranglers were getting to meet the riders and learning their horse-riding history and their comfort zone while "sizing up" the right horse for each rider.

During the process I would occasionally offer my encouragement, or my own opinion and my vast horse experience, or maybe some follow-up suggestions of ridership to help the wranglers. Maybe I talked too much. All the other riders were set and mounted, just waiting for us. I may have interrupted a few times when the girls were listening or talking to the wrangler. Finally, and lastly, I was introduced to my horse for the day. As I was being helped up to the saddle I asked the head man, "Wow, this is a great looking horse … what kind is it?" And before I could pick up the reins on the horse's neck or put my feet into the stirrups the wrangler said, so all could hear, "Why, that ain't no horse Mr. Cowboy, that's a jackass!" Simultaneously he swung a long 2 x 4 piece of wood with a hard homerun vengeance against the ass of the jackass who jolted forward into a half gallop or walk or trot or combination of all the above. He took me by surprise! All I could do to stay on the angry beast was to hang on with a two-handed white knuckle vice grip around the saddle horn, all while my feet were violently searching for the stirrups, as I raced through the laughing crowd and listening to the yells of my children. "Hang on Dad! You can do it!" Their tears appeared either from laughing at or embarrassment for me.

"We are like butterflies who flutter for a day and think that it is forever …"
—*Carl Sagan, American astronomer, and cosmologist*

---

* * *

In May, Jerry, Rik, Guy Kenny, and I drove to Sault Ste. Marie, Canada, and loaded our canoes and gear into the train's freight car to start Rik's and my second canoe trip down the Agawa River. It's over a three-hour train ride north into Ontario. The river is remote and rarely navigated; you are on your own. There is no designated campsites or signage (except for one). We planned our trip with two overnights, allowing time to explore and let the current do most of the work. Apparently, the spring was colder than normal because remnants of snow were still along some of the shady banks. This was Jerry's and Guy's first trip; Guy was an expert canoeist.

Jerry and I decided he would be in the rear seat to steer and paddle and I would look out for obstacles and danger from the front and that we would follow Rik and Guy. The initial easy rapids, in less than two feet of water, came up quick. We got sideways to the river's current that flooded our canoe. We had to jump out and unload our gear to drain it. A wet start, and you could still see the railroad tracks behind us.

During a stop for lunch Rik told us about the tough section of the river just around the upcoming bend. He warned us to stay close to shore on the right side of the river, and Guy told me, "Whatever you do, do not hold on to the edges of the canoe while in rapids, just go through them. Let Jerry paddle and steer like your life depended on it."

We followed close behind for a while and watched Guy maneuver with ease his canoe near the right side of the river. Jerry and I started, but the river decided to take a different approach for us, and before I could warn Jerry, we found ourselves riding up and over a large underwater shelf while at the same time dropping my paddle and holding on tight to the canoe's edges before it cartwheeled us up and over into the frigid river. I was under water on my back looking up, when I saw our empty canoe floating above me. Jerry and I scrambled our way to shore, and Rik retrieved the canoe while he and Guy laughed so loud, they could have stirred up the bones of a dead Indian. Note: Don't use your life jacket as a seat cushion.

I wasn't mad about swimming in 34-degree river water, but Rik and Guy continued laughing while we rounded up our gear and food and supplies. I was pissed off! How could good friends be so thoughtless, crude, and cruel?

The next morning was warm and sunny, and Jerry and I were almost dry. I can remember telling my brother that somewhere on the river is the one sign we need to see that signals danger. It has skull and crossbones on it and we should be on the constant look-out. We were just drifting with the river, enjoying its beauty and the warmth of the sun when we heard Rik and Guy shouting from upriver. Waving frantically from the shore for us to get to their safe side of the quickening river. We hadn't noticed the current's increased speed or the ripples. Jerry and I started paddling like our life depended on it. Like it did. But the current was strong and as we were about to pass them, Guy ran fast with his knees high through shallow rapids over the gravel bottom, grabbing our canoe and pulling us to the shore's safety.

Nobody laughed today. I told Rik that we did not see the danger sign. They didn't either; it must not have survived the winter. Guy noticed the speed of the river and heard the falls. We thanked them profusely and began the difficult portage, eventually seeing the 50-foot-tall waterfall with its talus of boulders and rocks and sharp-edged debris below it, before re-launching our canoes and continuing our trip. What are best friends for?

The decade was filled with hundreds of boating days. Each one was different and adventurous. In August of 2002, our grandson Jon Andrew joined us on our trip to the North Channel. If weather and time were in sync, we would usually stop at the Abandoned Lighthouse near the end of Waugoshance Point that marks the turn east toward the Mackinac Bridge to swim, so we did. The water there is spectacularly clear and young Jon reveled as he swam among the strewn boulders the size of refrigerators and busses.

Late that summer John Winn asked me to help him deliver two boats from Charlevoix to Racine, Wisconsin's fall boat show. Carol went with me on a 53' McKenna motor yacht and John drove a 47' McKenna. We stopped in Frankfurt for the night, with a prediction of high winds. The next day was still windy but forecasted for easing wind and moderate waves, so we started the crossing in the early afternoon. It began with fair weather but deteriorated midway and developed rather quickly into a Lake Michigan tempest. It was slow-going, fighting 6- to 10-ft waves from the northwest. We kept each other in sight and maintained radio contact all the way. The lake was so rough that on occasion we could see John's boat keel when hit broadside by an exceptionally large wave. Eventually the waves subsided, and the threatening lake settled before reaching the break wall to Racine Harbor in the dark with calm winds.

A few weeks later that summer, Jenifer and I picked up the same 53' McKenna at the Michigan City, Indiana, marina boat show and brought it back to Charlevoix via a nighttime arrival in St. Joseph where Joan and family came to see us and the boat.

Also, Lou Mettler, a local menswear store owner, who made it big with a store and restaurant in Naples, Florida, asked me to take his newly reconditioned wood Hatteras motor yacht christened *Ol' Hat* from Charlevoix to Chicago. Carol helped me sail it to St. Joseph where Lou had arranged a crew member to join me. Joan and her family again came over to see the boat and pick up Carol. It was an easy cruise until a dead calm and dense fog settled in all around us, restricting our sight lines to zero. I slowed her down to a quiet timid crawl. The radar did not work, so I blew the horn for five seconds every two or three minutes for over an hour until it gradually cleared, hoping a freighter could hear the horn or spot us on their working radar. That was creepy, but I still enjoyed the crossing.

*   *   *

It was about this time that I realized that we had more money than time; I began to slow down. My financial level of comfort and security was upon us, and my tolerance of risk had narrowed to a frightful hesitancy of inaction. Our assets had reached a level that would provide security to enjoy our current lifestyle and an emergency cushion for our growing family. I concluded that the need to pursue wealth was not worth the price. In hindsight it seemed so easy. Within a few years I stopped making phone calls and it wasn't long when the phone's ring became the days novelty. I settled into a busy life of pleasant insignificance and travel. My Northern Michigan Charlevoix construction days ended with over 175,000 square feet of development on Round Lake. A lasting mark on the cityscape of Charlevoix. It is an historical unmatched achievement by any other individual or company.

In the late fall of 2002, we purchased a slightly used 28' Coachman Class C Pathfinder RV motor home from a dealer in Traverse City. And on January 3, 2003, we departed Charlevoix on a crisp, cold morning to begin our nine-week, over 8,000-mile wandering motor home road trip. It eventually took us all the way down to Cabo San Lucas at the southernmost tip of Mexico's Baja Peninsula. We stopped at numerous remote beachside pull-overs on the shores of the Pacific or the Bay of California (Sea of Cortez). The motor home's suspension system was stretched to its limits so Carol sometimes had to walk in front, pointing the way to avoid deep ruts or wayward oversize rocks that somehow would show up in our path, that led us to a shore.

For a few days we camped on the beach near Los Todos on the Pacific Ocean. One afternoon we walked the few hundred

Bathhouse at our second stop in Baja, Mexico. The sign reads, "Please Do Not Allow Your Pet To Shit On Motel Grounds."

yards to the public beach where we were surprised to see Sara Gay and Tom Damman from Charlevoix (their son took Jenifer to the Junior prom). We were surprised by the remote coincidence, laughing and hugging. Tom was a retired national press correspondent who spent time in Europe, reporting on World War II from the beginning to its end. Tom knew of my interest in history and once asked me if I wanted to shake the hand of the hand that shook the hand of Adolf Hitler. Not really, but his hand was already reaching for mine.

Sara Gay was a freelance writer with connections to the Detroit daily newspapers. She had interviewed me in the past. That same afternoon Carol and I had a snack at the "Hotel California," made famous by the rock band the Eagles (not a favorite of mine) when we heard of the space shuttle *Columbia's* disintegration over East Texas on its descent. The seven brave astronaut's remains were scattered within a twenty-mile radius only 16 minutes from safely landing at Cape Canaveral, Florida.

During the trip I made arrangements with the Moorings to rent a 39' catamaran sailboat, sister ship to *Resolution,* for a week from their base in La Paz, Mexico. Jerry flew down to join us, and Jenifer and fiancé, Dave. Witham, drove about 40 miles south from their kite boarding camp in La Ventana. We sailed north into the Gulf of California, AKA Sea of Cortez, for a week. We anchored every night in secluded coves of clear water with nightly fresh-made orange margaritas, lots of exploring, snorkeling, and swimming. On one daytime adventure we anchored next to some small islands that were inhabited by hundreds of sea lions, sunbathing in their stink and making lots of sea lion noises.

In a short time, we were all in the water snorkeling between the boat and shore when I was greeted by a huge sea lion bull that came out of the deep from nowhere before putting his nose up to my face mask. Gulp. The island was soon almost empty as we swam among the mutually curious sea lions, each of us and them enjoying the experience.

After leaving La Paz on our way back to the States we stopped at Ensenada on the Pacific side of Baja where gray whales annually come to give birth. We were seated with four other guests on a small skiff, while the captain carefully guided us into the nursery area of the cove between humongous females and their calves. Carol and I were able to take part in a rare magical up-close encounter when we reached over and touched a gentle whale while staring directly into its wide-open softball-size eye only several inches away. Emotional, spiritual, mystical, and mesmerizing. One Soul To Another.

A few weeks after returning from Mexico, Carol and I flew to St. Maarten (our second visit) in the Leeward islands where we met Jessica, Jerry, his son Chad and his wife, Lindsay, (seven months pregnant) a few days later. While watching TV that night we witnessed the start of the Iraq war to topple the notorious Saddam Hussein's regime. The war was premised on a false intelligence report that the dictator had a stockpile of nuclear weapons. The war eventually became the catalyst for decades of chronic chaos within the Mideast, causing several hundred thousand civilian deaths, and the sacrifice of thousands of men and women in our armed forces and tens of thousands of severe injuries and several trillion dollars of US treasury. It's hard to imagine the horrific results of what misinformation and lies can cause. Beware of lies and misinformation.

Beware of lies and misinformation.

Whenever I think of St. Maarten, memories of one of my all-time favorite beaches in the world comes to mind. Not for its beauty or wide swaths of beautiful sand with towering palms, but because of its unique location at the very end of Princess Juliana International Airport runway. As soon as I heard the big jets taxi toward the beach, I would jump into the ocean and position myself in about six feet of water and wait for the planes to start their U-turn and ready the engines for takeoff to Europe or the States. Occasionally the pilots would return my wave to them with a smile. They appeared so close you could almost read their lips saying, "So long." Just as the captain started the jet engines full throttle and its ear-splitting roar, I would sink beneath the waves to protect myself from the dirty sand and small stones that would blow over me with the force of a strong hurricane. I had to hold a long breath until it was safe to surface. I enjoyed many hours of the day on that beach waiting for those takeoffs and landings, especially when treated to a wave of goodbye from the pilot. If you ever find yourself in St. Maarten, find the beach and enjoy the blast.

What a life; I become more grateful with each recovered memory. What luck, hallelujah!

During one winter Carol and I joined a local dive group in Cozumel, Mexico, an island off the coast of the Yucatan Peninsula, for a week. The unique dive experience was the steady four to five mph ocean current. You just folded up at a comfortable depth and rode the underwater highway, passing coral and fish along the route. The night dive was special and a little scary too, except it became Carol's last scuba dive. It's stressful enough to start a dive in the middle of the night, but add an equipment failure in the deep, and it can become awfully terrifying. Even more so after your husband puts things back to normal while buddy breathing in 45 feet of water and you find yourselves separated from the dive boat and all of the fellow divers. Luckily, we both saw a single waving flashlight in the distant dark ocean and started kicking our flippers toward it and safety.

Another dive I enjoyed was into a cave. Some of our dive group took the ferry across to the mainland where a van drove the six of us inland about 25 miles to a cenote (sinkhole). We had to descend a steep 20-foot, handmade ladder of bamboo and twine to the cave's opening. It was another magical and beautiful moment of memory. We each had a light and followed a guide in front, and one was in the back. My dive partner was inexperienced and should not have signed up for such a taxing dive. He followed me and soon developed trouble adjusting his buoyancy. I could tell because sometimes the bottom and the top of the cave was a little tight, but still plenty of room and I could hear the clink, clink, clink, every so often as he hit the top of the cave, damaging the ancient stalactite mineral formations. That's not good.

What's worse, at the end of the dive while waiting to climb out, I looked in my partner's eyes and it was ghastly. He had not neutralized his facemask pressure. It's so easy—you just exhale through your nose once in a while; it's actually quite natural. His eyes bulged out like they were going to pop out if he sneezed. It took a few days for the eyes to return to normal and I doubt that he ever dove again.

*   *   *

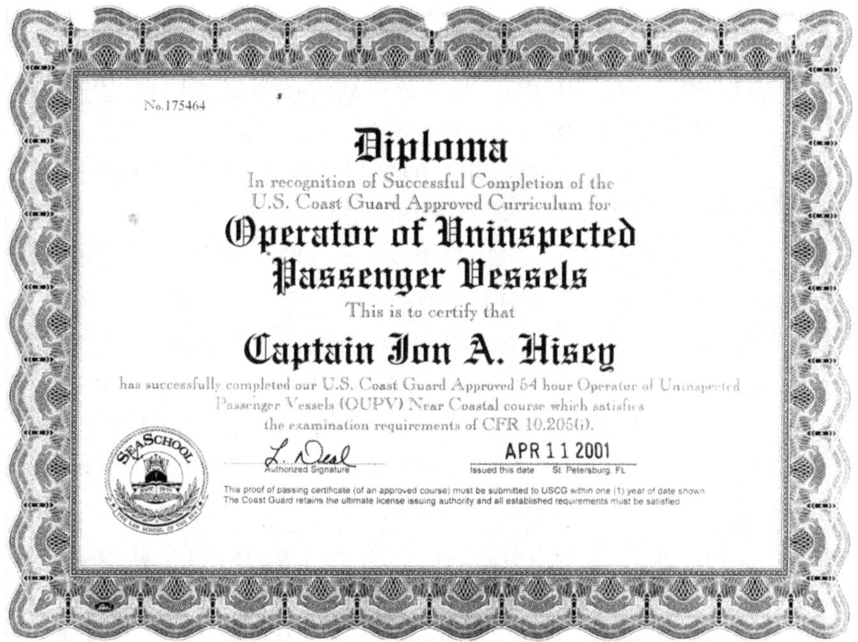

In late April of 2003, I was contacted by John Miller from Peoria, Illinois. He had purchased the big McKenna yacht that I had captained the previous year from Charlevoix to Racine, Wisconsin, and back. Mr. Miller was a wealthy junk dealer who had bought the boat directly from Bob Million, the owner of McKenna Yacht Company that I had met in Racine. John hired me to drive his boat from Lake Pontchartrain, New Orleans, up to Lake Peoria, IL. He approved my request to take Jenifer, Carol, and our friend Brownie Flanders who had made the trip once before on another boat.

Over the next few years, I shuttled the McKenna, north and south. After John sold the boat, he purchased a 47' Cruisers Inc. motor yacht for additional trips up and down the Mississippi River and the Ten Tom Waterway lock system. Coincidentally, he sold the McKenna to the founder of the Moorings, in Tortola, where *Resolution* was kept.

All northbound trips were in the spring and extraordinarily

difficult on the Mississippi portion of the trips because of consistent flood stage conditions. Once you turned north from the Ohio River at Cairo, Illinois, and into the Mississippi River, it was a 180-mile challenge against the current until you reach the convergence of the Illinois River at Alton, Illinois.

On my first trip north, as soon as we hit the Mississippi, the Mississippi hit us back with especially strong currents, one- to three-foot river waves accompanied with large dangerous debris including empty barrels, parts of trees, poles, and a refrigerator. Navigational aids and buoys had been misplaced or were missing, pulled down under by the river's swift current. Everyone was at the helm with me, using binoculars and expressing tense encouragement for several hours before the river's grip relaxed. We made it without a scratch. That was definitely good luck.

I loved each trip, especially the ones that included grandson Jon Andrew, Carol, Jen, Jon C, and Jerry, who was with me most of the time. Every day was filled with excitement, beautiful scenery. Eighty locks were strategically located between the south end of Lake Peoria, to the Illinois River where it converged to the Mississippi, the Ohio River, the Ten-Tom River system and ending with the last lock at Demopolis, Alabama, about 100 miles north of Mobile Bay. It included nightly stops at local marinas or anchoring when necessary, river restaurant shacks, and southern hospitality. It took about seven to ten days to complete each trip.

My last southbound trip included my son Jon and Jerry. We departed Peoria, Illinois, on John Miller's *Euphoria*, a 47' Cruisers Inc. motor yacht. We made pretty good time with the exception of over six hour waits on two of the locks because of heavy commercial barge traffic and then were delayed one and a half days in Panama City with an engine starter problem.

After repairs, we made a short cruise to Apalachicola located on the south shore in the middle of Florida's panhandle for the night. The three of us decided to make a run for the finish line in the morning. It was a straight diagonal course across the 215 miles of open water in the Gulf of Mexico to Longboat Key, our destination.

In the early morning, we cleared the harbor break wall and passed through the St. George Island government cut and into the Gulf just as the sun broke the easterly horizon, revealing the first blue light of the day's sky. A beautiful morning. The sea was still calm from the night's slack, just a slight breeze and a gentle roll. The three of us were on the bridge, mostly quiet, sipping black coffee while eating the last of the cookies for breakfast. I calculated a late afternoon arrival. Full throttle.

Midway we started to see patches of flotsam, mostly tight woven seaweed with sticks and pieces of rope "line" of various sizes. It caused us to slow down and maneuver around them while keeping a sharp lookout. Unfortunately, after a few hours of slow going I hit the edge of one and a piece of polypropylene (rope) wrapped tightly around the port engine's propeller shaft. In a few seconds, it automatically shut down. With only one engine our maximum speed was less than six mph before a robust vibration shook the whole boat. I knew we could not continue to Longboat Key but we might be able to make it to Clearwater before dark.

First, I decided to dive down to see what, if anything, we could do before turning east toward the distant coast. This boat, as was the McKenna, was used primarily for an occasional cocktail cruise; as a matter of fact, my personal ship's log showed only six to ten owner hours of engine time per season, compared to my shuttle service of about 90 to over 100 engine hours each way. There was no dive jacket, no diving mask, no snorkel, no goggles or swim fins, no sharp knives, not even a paring knife to cut limes. Nothing but a few butter knives and one small six-inch serrated utility knife.

As suspected, my exploratory dive confirmed that a line was tightly wound around a propeller shaft. *Phase III* déjà vu. Jerry and I began our task by one hand holding the knife with a firm grip and the other onto the shaft to steady yourself. You could only manage a few knife strikes against the line before resurfacing. We quickly rigged a dock line from one aft cleat, under the hull and up to the opposite deck cleat that allowed us an extra few seconds of down time by just pulling ourselves to and from the problem instead of using time and energy of kicking and swimming. Jerry and I took turns with the one six-inch knife, and used the cinched rope to pull ourselves quickly to the poly line and get several good knife swipes before returning back to the surface. Jon C. kept a lookout for sharks and helped us keep things moving. Each turn took about 15–20 seconds underwater. Normally I could easily hold my breath for a minute. The boat rode with the slight rhythm of the waves and it was difficult to keep our heads from banging the bottom of the boat. Dolphins and giant turtles came to watch strangers splashing amidst them. The 130 feet of ocean below us made us think of Great White sharks while adrenaline flowed like a five-alarm fire hose. Neither one of us could get past 20 seconds of down time. Jon was timing us as Jerry and I started some friendly brotherly competition.

After a long delay of this we were on our way to Longboat Key with a story to tell our grandchildren. At about 10:00 p.m., we were greeted by an anxious John Miller, his wife and Carol when we pulled into the marina.

Eric Shipton, an English Himalayan mountaineer said, "... such, after all, are the only possessions of which no fate, or luck, no cosmic catastrophe can deprive us; nothing can after the fact if for one moment in eternity we have really lived."

Another memorable boating episode of the decade was when we left Charlevoix in the morning of mid-September on our friend Don Jesmore's 31' Tiara boat, *True North* to Trenton, Ontario. The route took us through the North Channel down to Tobermory and then across Georgian Bay in a light rain with limited visibility to the start of Ontario's Trent-Severn canal system. It consisted of 40 different locks, rivers, lakes, and connecting canals to Lake Ontario. Don wanted the experience of bringing his boat back through the canals and locks to Charlevoix with his wife Ellen who had recently been diagnosed with Alzheimer's disease.

That cruise turned out to be one of our most lovely, enchanting, and favorite boat voyages to date. It was a trip back in time with quaint villages at each lock. Some locks were still operated by manually turning the large gear to open the gates. One was a railway "lock." You had to drive the boat onto an underwater crib and turn off the engines before the lock master started moving the boat up a small hill, then over train tracks and a one-lane road where waiting automobile occupants waved us on. You were gently moved downward to the next river's water level. And, at Peterborough lock there is the highest hydraulic lift "elevator" lock in the world. You entered into a big tub of water that lowered us down almost 60 feet to the next water level while simultaneously lifting up boats that were traveling in the opposite direction. It opened in 1904. A special place, a special time. Unexplainable—unforgettable.

On the afternoon of August 5, we arrived at Frazer Park Marina in Trenton at the mouth of Lake Ontario and waited for Don and Ellen's arrival by car. The next day Don asked me to stay on the boat for a few locks to teach Ellen the "ropes" and the procedures of locking. Ellen's diagnosis soon became evident to me, and I am sure Don's level of worry increased by the time Carol picked me up at the 6th lock with Don's car and started our drive home. Ellen's condition proved too much for them and they left the boat in Midland, Ontario, on the south side of Georgian Bay just southeast past the Severn lock. They rented a car and drove home to Charlevoix. At least Don got to experience the Trent-Severn canal system, stressful as it must have been.

* * *

On August 30, 2003 daughter Jenifer and David Witham were married in the afternoon on the shores of Lake Charlevoix at Don and Ellen's home. My most memorable moment of the beautiful wedding was at the ceremony's end. Previously, I had given the DJ a CD of Andrea Bocelli and Sarah Brightman's rendition of "It's Time To Say Goodbye." As people started to get up and mingle with small talk before leaving, I gave the signal to start the song and asked Jenifer for our last dance. Alone within a circle of family and guests, we danced until the music stopped. Jen and I were standing quietly and motionless—she wouldn't let go. She started to cry, I started to cry. She wouldn't let go. Nearly everybody's crying. After a few awkward moments Dave came up and gently pulled Jen away. Together they walked down the dock and settled into John and Zita Winn's antique wood boat that had just pulled up, on cue, to take the newlyweds to see a famous Lake Michigan sunset. They waved goodbye; they were gone, she was gone.

The next day, on Carol's birthday, Jen and Dave along with their dog Lou drove Don's rental car to Midland, Canada, to bring back Jesmore's boat. They spent their honeymoon with a fantastic leisurely cruise through the North Channel back to Charlevoix.

Later that fall Carol and I flew to London to see the sights and walked among the historical landmarks that I had read so much about. We navigated the city by using the world's oldest and famous subway, "The Tube." The only time we used one of their iconic black taxis is when we dressed up to attend a concert at Royal Albert Hall that Queen Victoria had built to honor her late husband. We had no reservations, so I went up to the ticket counter to see what, if any, seats were available. It was almost a full house and we ended up, with another great amount of luck, front row balcony, stage right at a discounted price. As we started to chat with the guests next to us, we soon realized that we were talking to royalty from the country of Jordan. The featured performer was Sarah Brightman, and her last song of the evening was naturally, "It's Time to Say Goodbye." Isn't it amazing. You can't make this stuff up. Luck.

The next day we rented a car and drove a few hundred kilometers to Bath, England, a beautiful city that was first settled by the Romans, where they built a palatial hot springs bath house at its center. We also toured Stonehenge; Oxford University, the oldest university in the English-speaking world; and other iconic landmarks.

We returned to the States on board the elegant, well-mannered and prestigious 36-year-old, *Queen Elizabeth II* ocean liner. We sailed from Southampton to New York City, the same route as the *Titanic* except we arrived safely at dawn as the captain slowly maneuvered under the Verrazano-Narrows Bridge, clearing it by what seemed like only a few feet. Carol and I stood on the top deck, cold from the night, but warm from exhilaration as we turned up into the Hudson River and watched the lights of New York City start to intermittently extinguish with the tempo of the rising sun.

Another memorable sight of an extraordinary life. A gift.

*　*　*

On May 4, 2004, our loveable granddaughter Jenevieve Grace Witham was born in Salt Lake City, Utah. That summer we drove the RV to Jenifer and Dave's house in Kamas, Utah, a little town east of Park City. Granddaughter Julia had been there a few weeks helping her aunt with the new baby. After a few days Julia joined Carol and me for our return trip to Charlevoix. We spent about a week enjoying the sights along the way. We camped every night, except at Yellowstone National Park where we stayed in the historic 100-year-old Old Faithful Inn next to the geyser. We camped next to Lake Jenny in Idaho. We rafted the Snake River in Wyoming; saw a rodeo in Cheyenne; and visited Mt. Rushmore in the Black Hills of South Dakota before driving just seventeen miles to see the uncompleted Crazy Horse Mountain monument.

On the 8th of August, 2004, our daughter Jessica married David Levy on a beautiful day at the Perry Hotel in Petoskey, Michigan, on the outside terrace that overlooked Little Traverse Bay. It's a memorable day when you are obliged to give your last daughter away. A dual ceremony of Jewish and Christian traditions was woven together. My youngest beautiful daughter, radiant from the afternoon sun, and I slow danced in the center of a circle of many family and friends to Louis Armstrong's 1967 classic iconic ballad, "What a Wonderful World." Yes, it is.

* * *

Another trip in the decade was in February 2005 when we traveled with our friends Brownie and Susan Flanders to South Africa. Our trip included a jungle safari with a private guide. We camped in a tent that included a shower and toilet, a queen-size bed with a TV and remote. Some tent. Several times in the middle of the night a herd of flatulent zebras would wake us up as they ran noisily between our tents.

While in Johannesburg, Jessica was able to track us down in our hotel and sadly informed me that my dad took his last breath while driving alone in Gaylord, Michigan for some unknown reason. It was a mystery of circumstances of what, why, when, and where. Typical for Dad. He always said that he wanted to die with his boots on. Jerry had decided to wait until we returned to have his funeral in Charlevoix.

After the safari we flew to Victoria Falls, one of the seven wonders of the natural world, on the border of Zimbabwe and Zambia, where we rented an old helicopter with a young pilot to view the spectacular falls. While in Africa's east coast near Durban, our guide arranged a reef dive for me in the Indian Ocean. Regrettably this became my last ocean dive, and was completely opposite of my first dive some 25 years ago in the British Virgin Islands. It was a total humiliating and embarrassing event. It started with me telling the scuba shop manager all of my extensive experiences and showing him my old, faded YMCA dive card. He handed me all of my gear, and a few minutes later with the help of Carol and Brownie, "Hey," I said to the clerk," my dive suit doesn't fit." His smirk reply, "You put it on backwards."

I hustled down to the waiting boat carrying all my gear. It was a large rubber pontoon raft, already filled with other divers in their twenties to early thirties, just waiting for me. The pontoons seemed huge, over two feet in diameter and already floating next to the beach. I threw my gear in the last clear spot and then failed to hoist myself into the boat. After a few attempts a young couple grabbed me under my arms and lifted me into the boat headfirst. On the way to the coral reef dive spot, the dive master shouted, "Hey, look we are in a pod of dolphins! Does anybody want to swim and snorkel with them? Splash—the boat emptied before I could even put my fins on and when I jumped in, I realized my mask was on my forehead and grabbed it just as it came off. As I finished clearing my mask of water and adjusting the snorkel, my fellow companions were starting to reboard the raft. Of course, I knew how to get back on the boat's side from the water. Kick crazy hard while lifting yourself with the safety straps at the same time. I've done it dozens of times. I couldn't get back in the boat. This time I had to be lifted onto the raft by a girl in good shape wearing an unzipped dive jacket and a skimpy two-piece red bathing suit and a boy from France, I don't remember much of how he looked.

When we arrived at our destination, I was fit and ready. A nice backroll entry in about 50 feet of clear ocean over a majestic field of coral. Ahhh—back into my element. On my slow descent I noticed my ears didn't equalize. I did all of the usual steps, even doing somersaults; nothing seemed to work. I could see the group congregating on the bottom waiting for me. I completed the dive while the pain of my ears felt like they were dangling from the side of my head. Very, painful. Not smart. One fateful memory of an ending from a field of many delightful underwater adventures.

* * *

On July 24, we departed Charlevoix for the North Channel at 11:00 a.m. with 9½-year-old grandson Clarke, and made our normal stops, including Croker Island, the Benjamins, the Pool at the end of the Baie of Finn, and hiking to Lake Topaz to swim and jump off the cliffs. With an unusual amount of happy hour laughter, we continued to Killarney, and ate whitefish with chips with malt vinegar (French fries) from the red dockside school bus. We stopped at Mackinac Island on the return trip to swim on the island's east side where the smooth limestone shelf warmed the water.

On the go again, we packed our carry-on bags and flew to the coast of southern Spain where we were to meet Joan, her first trip to Europe. Unfortunately, her adventure started with day-long flight delays connecting London to Madrid and to our airport at Malaga. Carol and I waited and worried for over 8 hours. Joan was with us for 6 of our 10-day trip to the Malaga coast that included a ferry across the Mediterranean to Morocco in northern Africa. We rented a car and toured the working studio and museum of Picasso, the Palace Alhambra in Granada and drove inland to Ronda, one of Spain's oldest cities. We toured its famous bullfighting ring where Ernest Hemingway saw his last bullfight. Tradition says the sport originated here (if you call bullfighting a sport).

Around Christmas every year, while I was in Charlevoix, it was customary for Rik L., John W., and I to meet at the Weathervane Bar for some holiday cheer. John happened to tell us about a visit he had recently made to Grand Bay Marine, just outside of Holland, Michigan. He described to us about a big yacht for sale that he had seen in one of the marina's heated storage buildings. John extolled about the boat's size and its great engines, two generators, and a stand-up engine room. It had all the bells and whistles that one could ever imagine, and he was thinking about buying it with a lowball offer of $225,000. "Wow!" I said, "that seems awfully cheap for a boat like that."

The next month, I flew to Grand Rapids from Florida to meet John and Rik at Grand Isle Marine. When Rik and I first saw the boat, we couldn't believe how big it looked, the biggest boat in the building. Frankly, I was hooked, falling back into my hypnotic state of irrational thinking when a boat is close, but able to reign in my early enthusiasm. It was 61' long plus it had a large swim platform and a two-foot bowsprit that carried two heavy anchors. It had a 13-foot Boston Whaler with a 150 HP engine mounted on the aft deck roof with an electric hoist. There were two- and one-half heads (nautical term for bathrooms), full galley, dishwasher, bow thrusters, hydraulic stabilizers, two sets of electronics, two TVs, washer, dryer, three staterooms, everything one can imagine and then some. It even had a meat locker in the stern lazaret, a bridge with a helm station and one on the main level, and a capacity of 1200 gallons of diesel fuel for extended cruising. Rik was reluctant because of the size but I quickly convinced him that a boat like this would be easier to drive and maneuver than my 39' Sea Ray. John begged out; he thought three partners would be a complicated mess, and I didn't think John wanted it in his boathouse on Round Lake with two other owners.

Rik and I decided to put in an offer of $225,000 cash. And within ten minutes the salesman came back after talking to the owner and said that offer would be a waste of time. We looked at John, "What about the $225,000 you talked about"? He just shrugged his shoulders. Later that week Rik and I made a new offer of $250,000 with the absolute understanding that this would be our last and final offer. Absolutely, positively last offer. After a few days, Rik and I formed a new partnership and bought the boat for $275,000. They say three's a charm, right? Wrong. How on earth could I have possibly let myself buy another super-sized boat? Rik came up with the idea to rename her *Two Choices* (Jon or Rik). I wanted to name it *Irrational*.

Our plan was to keep *Two Choices* at my dock at Edgewater Inn and lease it out with the benefit of my captain's license. We would cruise to the North Channel for a few summers and then drive her down to Florida with the idea of selling it at a huge profit.

* * *

Our last grandson, Charles Jon Witham was born on Monday, March 27, 2006, in Salt Lake City. At Jessica and David's request I designed their new home that was built on a large lot within the Charlevoix Country Club. The property was enhanced by a pond. Soon after the house was complete, I began to really enjoy the challenge and several days of hands-on hard work to design and build a water feature. It included a pool, waterfall, and meandering stream that was made from two truckloads of boulders and stones I purchased in the Upper Peninsula.

Our next trip overseas began with a flight to Cairo, Egypt, a city of antiquities, where we met Brownie and Susan Flanders. Of course we visited the Sphinx, the pyramids, and walked down a narrow tunnel into King Tut's decorative burial chamber. A short flight south delivered us to the famous Aswan Dam to begin our five-day cruise downstream on the Nile River back to Cairo. We then flew to Amman, Jordan, and hired a private taxi for a long drive into the night before reaching the heavily guarded Jordan/Israel border where our next prearranged guide picked us up. We continued the trip to Jerusalem, arriving at our hotel late that night. We spent a week touring the area of Jerusalem and its kosher restaurants where I stirred up quite a kerfuffle when I asked for a single slice of cheese to transform my hamburger into a cheeseburger. In a small shop next to the Church of Calvary, I bought an authentic (kind of), expensive, (sort of) 2000-year-old Roman coin and had it set into a necklace for Carol. The kindly elderly Jewish salesman suggested that perhaps Christ himself might have touched this coin. Sounded good to me.

We walked the seven stations of Christ to the church built over the site of his crucifixion, and looked into the tomb where Christ's body was laid on a slab of the chiseled rock crypt. The next day we wound our way through a maze of high concrete walls where young armed Israeli guards with automatic rifles stood at every turn. We emptied into Bethlehem, Palestinian territory and to the church that was built above the presumed site of Christ's birth. Bethlehem was a sad place and seemed deserted compared to the hustle and bustle of Jerusalem. Our guide took us to Nazareth and the Jordan River, where Brownie collected "Holy" water for baptisms in his church. We floated in the salty Dead Sea and toured the isolated mountaintop fortress of Masada and the Mediterranean coast to Tel Aviv.

* * *

On May 30, 2006, Rik, Buck Bradley, Denny Heck, and I boarded the 61' Halverson Island Gypsy at Grand Isle Marine and began our cruise back to Charlevoix with an overnight stop in Frankfurt. The next day we nestled her (only a few inches to spare between the port and starboard pilings) into her new home in my slip at the Edgewater Inn around 2:30 in the afternoon.

In mid-July we began our first trip to the North Channel on *Two Choices* with nine people on board for the cruise to Detour, Michigan, for our first night. The next morning five people disembarked and with Carol, Jerry, and granddaughter Jenica we continued our trip on our way to the Benjamin Islands. The first anchorage was in the bay between the North and South Benjamins when we noticed threatening clouds in the west and began to monitor the Canadian weather channel. To be extra cautious we decided to put out the second bow anchor and its heavy chain by using the dinghy. Soon after the anchor was safely set (after I did my customary visual with my snorkel and mask), a rented sailboat from Gore Bay arrived and, strangely enough, dropped its anchor between us and the shore. I made my way to the bow and leaned forward from the bowsprit and began to politely tell them that they were too close and should move either forward or off to our starboard side. It was at this moment that a storm struck with such speed and force I had to literally hang on and crawl my way back to the lower helm station. The two anchors and chains looked strained, so I started both engines and put them in forward gear with some throttle.

The rain and wind were horrendous, and I can remember Jenica coming up to me and asking in a worried voice, "Grandpa, are we going to be okay"? "Yes, Jenica I'm sure we will be fine but ask me again in 15 minutes." In hindsight that didn't sound very comforting. While that exchange was going on Carol screamed, "Look!" The small sailboat with two inexperienced elderly souls onboard came loose and was being blown straight back toward us. Bang! They hit the bowsprit on our port side. Bang! It scraped our port gunnels as the man in the runaway sailboat looked aghast at us for a second with two huge, wide-open eyes and a face expressing total fear. He cleared our stern and immediately was thrown into a 360 rotation over our dinghy and its engine. He continued whiplashing before disappearing into the raging storm behind us. After about 10 terrible minutes the storm ended almost as quickly as it started. The Boston Whaler and engine were still attached to its line and the boat's cleat but was barely floating with the load of rain and the storm's surf waters. The runaway sailboat was not in sight. We were afraid that the worst might have happened. We all went topside to check things out and discovered that our top canvas had been shredded and destroyed. The wind speed indicator had disappeared, but the instrument display panel was stuck at 115 miles per hour. Jerry and I bailed the Whaler out and got the engine started. We toured the harbor talking to other boaters and helped a few stray boats pull from the shore. It was eerily calm, quiet, and serene. It was later that day the four of us surveyed the South Island and saw trees that must have been over 100 years old uprooted, leaving holes of sand, rocks, and torn roots. The microburst was big news in Canada and resulted in several million dollars of damage on Manitoulin Island.

That afternoon we motored to Gore Bay and checked in with the Canadian Yacht Charter Co. to see if they had contact from the elderly couple on the sailboat that they rented. He reported that they heard from the couple after the storm and had sent their men in a chase boat to get them and one of our crew members brought the

Two Choices anchored off Snug Harbor in the North Channel.

sailboat back. He went on to say that this was the couple's first time on a rented sailboat, and it was the wife's birthday gift to the husband. They were lodged and resting in the local motel. I doubt that they ever set foot on a sailboat again. We then surveyed the damage done to our boat and made arrangements for them to fix it at their cost.

From Gore Bay we sailed (motored) to Little Current, a small town on the north shore of Manitoulin Island on the river between the east and west portions of the North Channel. It is where we would typically spend a night and add some fuel and provisions and treat ourselves to a double-dipped ice cream cone after dinner and pick up or drop off passengers. It was here that Joan, Clarke, and Claire joined us and Jerry drove Joan's car back to Charlevoix. We were eager to share highlights of our adventures with them.

It was a real treat to have Joan and three of our grandchildren together as we laughed, swam, and jumped from the high, top deck on our way through our favorite anchorages, watching their reactions of wonder and joy. A month of cruising. *Two Choices* is a fantastic live-aboard yacht. Rik occasionally joined us as his schedule permitted and spent a few days with his son, Austin, during this channel cruise.

*   *   *

I can vividly recall the time when Jenifer asked me to come to Park City and help her fly three-year-old Jenevieve and grandson Charles Jon (Charlie), who was a few weeks shy of his first birthday, to Florida. She was terrified by the thought of flying without help with such young children. Of course, I took the opportunity to ski a few days before our day to fly to Ft. Myers. It started with a 3:30 a.m. wake up for a 6:00 a.m. departure. At the check-in security line, I began to feel a little queasy. My seat was in the exit row next to a frail elderly (very old) lady, and Jenifer and children were seated one row back on the opposite side. Before I buckled up, I took a few steps back to check on Jen and whispered, "I hope my seatmate makes it through." Jen looked up while fastening Jenevieve's seatbelt and holding Charlie on her knees, "Yeah—I hope she does too," then returned to her children's chores.

High above the Rockies, maybe a third of the way to Atlanta, I began to feel uncomfortable. I was heating up, had some light-headedness and an urgent need to use the toilet. Luckily its door was in sight, only a few steps away. I tried the door. It was locked. I remember turning to see Jenifer return my glance and faintly heard her piercing scream, "Dad!" Slam, Boom, Bang, down I went right in front of the door, flat faced against the floor's dirty carpet. When I finally came to, I was surrounded by several flight attendants. The first thing I heard was from someone near the rear of the plane shouting, "IS HE DEAD!?"

They rolled me onto my back and placed a pillow under my head and I could see little Jenevieve with both hands clenched on the back of the seat ahead of her with big, wide-opened eyes of concern staring at her grandpa on the floor. A retired EMS technician tried to insert an IV saline solution into a vein. She inserted two different needles in two different veins without success. A pediatrician came to the mix and tried the last saline solution on board before giving up and telling me I had pretty tough veins compared with youngsters she usually dealt with. Three and out. The head stewardess had been keeping the pilots apprised of the situation and asked me, "Are you feeling good enough to continue to Atlanta or does the captain need to declare an emergency and divert to Tulsa because the window to Tulsa is fast approaching." I told her that we'd better keep going. Better to take my chances to Atlanta rather than be killed by a mob of angry passengers.

I laid on the floor until the plane started its descent to Atlanta.

The feeble nice old lady had already moved from her seat to help Jenifer with Charlie. She was a big help. They placed me in a fetal position on the empty seats and buckled me up. There was a wheelchair at the gate with two medical personnel. They checked my vitals, and cleared me for our next flight, then helped us make our connection to Ft. Myers.

My trip to Utah to help my daughter ended with Carol near the baggage claim carousel watching Jenifer push my wheelchair with one hand while carrying Charlie on her hip and little Jenevieve trying to help push the other chair handle, and me slouched in the wheelchair hugging my carry-on and Jenifer's big baby duffle bag. My spring golden ski tan had turned to a whiter shade of pale. Jenifer has never asked me again to help travel with my precious grandchildren.

* * *

On the Friday morning of June 29th, 2007 our last granddaughter, Jaydee Louise Levy was born in Charlevoix, Michigan. She had a big smile of welcome. Later that year Carol and I flew to Seattle, Washington, and spent two nights with Chuck and Mardell Witham (Jenifer's in-laws) at their home on Bainbridge Island. From there they drove us up to Townsend, Washington, where we boarded the ferry for a short ride across the Strait of Juan de Fuca to Victoria, Canada, for a few days. Another ferry took us for a long ride back to Seattle for several more days that included a fast elevator ride up to the top of the city's iconic Space Needle, a repeat of my 1965 trip. We also toured the huge Boeing airplane assembly plant, the largest building in the world by volume that sits on about 100 acres in Everett. To save money and for fun we took a public bus with all of its 20 to 30 stops to the Seattle/Tacoma International airport on the way back to Charlevoix.

One trip worth mentioning in 2008 was when Carol and

I returned to Hong Kong by joining a group of Winter Haven, Florida, Rollins College graduates. On the way to Detroit Metro Airport from Charlevoix we stopped to visit Carol's mother, Marian, in East Lansing who was in failing health. We needed to say our goodbyes. She passed away the following Friday, May 30 at 95 years old.

We met our Florida neighbor friend Beverly and Janet Taht (Beverly's sister-in-law) in Los Angeles that evening. The next afternoon we flew to Hong Kong and then to Beijing. We then sailed, flew, bullet trained, and bussed our way throughout China for three busy weeks. We saw and walked the Great Wall, the famous and recently discovered Terra Cotta Soldiers, cruised the Yangtze River, and went through the engineering marvel of the Three Gorges Dam, the world's largest hydroelectric facility.

We wandered Shanghai's bustling famous Waterfront area called the Bund, where I became distracted and stopped a pick-pocket by grabbing a young, and beautiful girl's hand from my back pants pocket. China is a paradox of contradictions. The major cities are defined by seemingly empty modern skyscrapers designed by the world's winning architects. Urban areas are bordered by family farms next to high-speed bullet trains while old men and women still use oxen to pull their ancient plows.

*   *   *

On September 1st, 2009, at 9:30 a.m., Charlevoix's iconic bridge raised for the passage of *Two Choices* for the final time to begin her one-way cruise south to Florida. Rik and Jerry joined Carol and I as we traveled through the North Channel and into Georgian Bay before reaching the Port Trent-Severn lock system again. Construction began in 1833 and finished in 1928. Its 240 miles and 44 locks cut through Ontario, saving hundreds of miles and days from the alternate route of sailing down to the bottom of Lake Huron, past Detroit, and through Lake Erie and into the Welland Canal.

In the first lock (and smallest) we had to literally squeeze her in by angling into the lock's opposite corners before the lockmaster could close the back doors. The lockmaster said that he thought we were the largest boat of the year. After a stop in Trent, we crossed Lake Ontario to Oswego, New York, where Rik disembarked. The three of us then traversed the Erie Canal to Waterford, New York, at the junction of the Hudson River where we were rejoined by Rik with his two children Alexandra and Austen. We spent the next several days sailing down the Hudson River south to New York City and past the magnificent Statue of Liberty before entering into the marina next to Ellis Island. Rik and his children spent a few days with us before they made their way back to Charlevoix. After the weather finally cleared, Carol, Jerry, and I sailed under the Verrazano-Narrows Bridge early in the morning mist and into the forbidding Atlantic Ocean.

Late that afternoon we tied up on the marina's wall in Atlantic City. Ron and Beverly Taht came to visit, then drove us to their favorite restaurant and to their condominium in Ocean City where we slept that night in a motionless regular land bearing bed. From

Circling the Statue of Liberty from the deck
of *Two Choices.*

Atlantic City we sailed to Cape May, New Jersey, where we turned inward from the ocean to the intercoastal waterway. From there we continued south to Annapolis, Maryland, and into the large Chesapeake Bay. On our last morning in the bay, we entered a channel that would take us under the high I-64 bridge. On our port side we observed the Norfolk Naval Station, the United States' largest naval base, possibly in the world. We were minding our own business when two Navy chase boats approached us from the east head-on at full speed with flashing lights and sirens blaring. One had a large caliber machine gun mounted on its bow with an able-bodied seaman pointing it directly at us. The other boat came beside us and with a bullhorn (he was so close I think I could have heard him in a whisper), demanding us to immediately turn to port! At the same time Jerry shouted in a panic and pointed, "LOOK! LOOK! LOOK!" Looking aft we saw a coning tower and a little bit of its threatening forward black hull pushing a huge nuclear submarine wave less than a football field away, chasing us! That was very frightening and very memorable. For the rest of the voyage, we spent a lot of time closely monitoring our two marine radios, listening for the US Navy's urgent alerts.

Early that evening, we had to wait two hours for a drawbridge, before arriving at the Atlantic Yacht Basin, in Norfolk, Virginia, on October 2 to lay up *Two Choices* for the remainder of the hurricane season.

* * *

On November 29, 2009 at 10:30 a.m., a Saturday, Carol, Jerry, and I departed the Atlantic Yacht Basin to begin the next and last portion of our cruise to Jensen Beach, Florida. In North and South Carolina, we anchored in secluded bays or tributaries and marinas.

When in Georgia I vividly remember a late afternoon when the

Our 50th wedding anniversary
family photo.

winds were picking up when I radioed a nearby harbor master to confirm that the marina had a slip big enough to accommodate a vessel the size of *Two Choices,* and that we would need help with the quickening wind. As soon as we entered the second break wall, I knew this was going to be tough. The marina was too small to make a safe 180-degree turn. I could see a group of men waving to us at the end of a dock midway into the marina. Typically, when docking, you always approach into the wind or current for control. We lacked that option. *Two Choices* had no choice. We were docking with a strong wind behind us. I told Jerry we are only going to have one chance in our approach into the slip and to fetch the long heavy line. I pointed the bow at the upwind piling at the dock's end and got so close Jerry could almost hand them the rope. The men quickly wrapped the line around the starboard's first piling, the strong wind almost immediately carried our eighty-thousand-pound boat's stern sideways and slammed into the portside piling about mid ship, causing the piling to permanently lean. Slowly we inched our way up into the slip and safety. It was too small for *Two Choices* and there wasn't any room for fenders. It was a good thing the first line held, avoiding a marine mess with lots of consequences from us running over several small boats in the marina. This memory of docking was the most harrowing of our trip. We were all wound up pretty tight until Carol remembered the bottle of bourbon. Not exactly another day at the office.

We reached Florida on December 9 and spent the night anchored close to the intercoastal channel in a Creek. That's my dream; in the middle of nowhere, secured by the anchor, sitting on the top deck with a sweater and staring into the magical night sky. We spent the next 5 days on the intercoastal before passing Cape Canaveral and finally arriving at Four Fish Marina at Jensen Beach at 2:15 p.m. Sunday, December 14, 2009. Frankly, relieved is the emotion that first comes to mind, when I stepped off the dock and kissed the dry Mother Earth.

Two Choices traveled 2510 statute miles from Charlevoix to Jensen Beach. It took 288 engine hours and used 2160 gallons of diesel fuel at an average cost of $3.07 per gallon. The total trip cost including fuel, dockage, maintenance, repairs, and two months of storage at Atlantic Yacht Basin and one month rent at Four Fish Marina was $15,500. This did not include insurance, food and beverage, or ground transportation. We sold her in the recession of 2010 in Ft. Lauderdale for $175,000 a huge loss, a cost worth every dollar. *Phase III, Engenuity, Resolution, Two Choices*; four wonderful boating chapters of my life. Priceless.

---

*I used to say that you can justify anything if you try hard enough . . .
even murder if you try.*

---

* * *

In June we flew to Vancouver, Canada, to start our eight-day Alaskan cruise on the Island Princess. Carol and I disembarked in Whittier, Alaska, and took a short train ride to Anchorage, where I tried to revisit my 1965 trip. We rented a car and drove the same route on the Glennallen Highway that I had hitched a ride to the Eureka Lodge where the big bear was 44 years ago.

We had the cheeseburgers and coke, but the bear was gone. I asked our waitress what happened to the big bear off the alcove on the way to the toilets. She replied. "Huh? What bear?" I said I was here in 1965 and there was a huge stuffed bear standing tall with his big mouth wide open and its big paws with long claws reaching up ready to kill you. "Folks, I'm only 19 and there isn't anyone older than 50 here." She returned a few minutes later and gave me a name and phone number of the current owner. "Call her, she might be able to help you with that bear thing."

We spent the night nearby in a small cabin motel, and after returning to Anchorage, we took the train north to Fairbanks. I asked some of the crew if they knew of a conductor named Don Prince who worked on the train many, many years ago. No one ever heard of him. The railroad hotel I had stayed in was gone, just an empty field of junk and scrub. I couldn't find my friendly restaurant. Author Thomas Wolfe said, "You can't go home again." I tried. He was right. You have to keep moving. You can't sit and wait. You can't dwell on the past, (except when you try and write about your past.) You have to keep moving, moving forward.

On the train back we did a stay over at the Denali Mountain National Park and took a ten-passenger plane, with me in the copilot seat (I told him before boarding that I had taken flying lessons when I was young), up and over the 20,300-foot mountain, on an unusually clear and calm day. We had to suck oxygen out of a small plastic tube, like a straw. The pilot tipped the wings to wave at some mountain climbers just a few hundred feet below us as they approached the summit. We were ecstatic, I'm sure the climbers were too. The pilot said these kind of days were an extreme rarity for Denali, maybe only a dozen in the whole year. It was a breathtaking, beautiful flight from start to finish. What luck.

Immediately after our return from Alaska we started construction on our cottage that I designed for 8400 Eastern Avenue in Pine Point near Lake Charlevoix. We had concluded the sale of Unit 212 at Harbour Plaza and Don Jesmore reached out to us to offer his home on Lake Charlevoix until we returned to Florida.

THE 2010s

DAYS OF MORE TRAINS, MORE PLANES, MORE AUTOMOBILES, BOATS, AND BUSES

THE DECADE OF 2010 BROUGHT THE PHENOMENON of social media's world influence into focus with mass unsettling protests. Demonstrations begging change in the Mideast countries and popular movements in the US flourished. My life's interest and one-time professional goal of teaching American history, political science and current events became almost insatiable in the run-up to the 2016 presidential election of Donald Trump and his first of two impeachment trials. His presidency fostered the expansion or amplification of the far right's antisemitism, racism, conspiracy theories, and most importantly, distrust of our government's institutions, i.e., Courts, FBI, IRS, EPA, CDC, and, most unfortunately, each other. History will not be kind to this president. A vast majority of historians have already concluded that he will go down as American's most inept, corrupt, deficient, and defiant president among all the other 44 men to occupy the White House.

A stain that will be hard to remove. It wasn't supposed to be like this.

Shortly after I had completed a draft of my memories, America witnessed the worst attack on our fragile democracy since the Civil War. Donald Trump actually attempted to violently overturn the 2020 presidential election and overthrow the presidency of Joe Biden. Republican leadership decided not to impeach him for the attempt, which would have swiftly swept him into history's infamous dust bin. Remember Nixon and Gore? Another day of "infamy" in my lifetime. Lincoln said, "As a nation of freemen, we must live through all time, or die by suicide."

"The price good men pay for indifference to public affairs is to be ruled by evil men."
—Plato

The ramifications of climate change fostered severe hurricanes, tornadoes, mega storms, and acute droughts and floods. Unfathomable mass shootings of school children and innocent citizens continued to bleed Americans into helpless despair. Paradoxically, the world was witnessing an unparalleled technological progress.

On a lighter note, my family continued its good health and providence with the addition of great grandchildren. Carol and I enjoyed our days of curious travel and experiencing different environments and cultures around the world. Music, movies, and TV were streaming on over 300 million smart phones worldwide. Our population had grown to 310 million, and the 99-year-old Wonder Bread had approached $2.00.

* * *

In January 2010, I attended a live concert at the Barbara Mann auditorium in Ft. Myers. It was a space-themed film orchestrated event that space shuttle astronaut Story Musgrave was going to narrate. Before show time I was sitting at a small table in the concession area near the lobby sipping a free punch and munching on a small cup of cashews when NASA astronaut Musgrave casually pulled out a chair next to me and sat down. I recovered quickly and held out my hand to introduce myself. We talked for a while before he soon realized my lifelong interest in American space history and my collection of astronaut autobiographies and autographs. He said, "Wait here a minute Jon," and returned with his autobiography, *The Way of Water*, written with Anne Lenehan. He then inscribed and gifted me his book and said, "Nice talking to you Jon, enjoy the show." As he was leaving, an announcement was heard that it was time to take your seats. That was lucky.

On my birthday we moved into our new "Cottage," and later that summer we launched *Engenuity* for the first time since the spring of 2005. All systems checked out, even the gas was still useable.

For Thanksgiving, we drove to Ft. Lauderdale from the Cape for a cruise to the Panama Canal on the Coral Princess (a sister ship of our Alaskan voyage). We stopped at Aruba and Columbia, before entering the canal and anchoring in its middle Gatun Lake. From there we continued on through the lock system on a smaller boat to Panama City and the Pacific Ocean, then back to the Island Princess. We then sailed to Costa Rica where we toured its beautiful mountainous countryside with huge banana plantations. Next was on to Ocho Rios, Jamaica, where Carol and I returned to climb Dunn's River Falls where we had previously scaled the rivers ledges over 44 years earlier in 1966.

Our next excursion into a new world of ancient cultures was in the spring of 2011 when we flew to Lima, Peru, to meet the Flanders to start our eleven-day trip, that included a stop in Cusco, the traditional starting point to visit the Peruvian UNESCO World Heritage site, Machu Picchu. A short train ride delivered us to the base of the 15th-century Incan empire citadel. We walked among the artfully and miraculously placed huge chunks of chiseled granite, within and on top of an 8,000-ft-high Andes Mountain ridge. It continues to amaze me how our ancient humans built humongous lasting structures with just ingenuity and brute strength. We then were bussed for nearly eight hours through the beautiful Amazon Basin to the small city of Puno and Lake Titicaca for our two-night visit. It is the highest freshwater lake in the world at 12,500 feet, located within the Andes. Our guide directed us to the "floating" fishing villages on the lake, where the indigenous people built their shelter huts from millions of lake reeds woven tightly together. We mingled among the natives and their children who support their standard of living by selling crafts and souvenirs. When we walked on the matted reeds, it was very wet, soft, and squishy. The world is full of amazing natural and human wonders of all different shapes, sizes, colors, and languages. Except the smiles. Everyone knows a smile, and everyone knows the word "please" and everyone knows "thank you." I suggest that you use all these as much as you can in all your travels, all the time. Smiles are the same everywhere; they are the language that says friendship, peace, and kindness.

We have all heard the phrase, "It's a small world." For example, Lake Titicaca is remote, over 4200 miles between Michigan and the high lake. One could say, "You can't get there from here." On our last night on the top of the Andes Mountain range, the four of us were in town looking for a small restaurant that served the local popular dish of a baked, completely intact guinea pig including eyes and face, within walking distance of our hotel. Susan always liked to experience the local cuisine in our travels together. Brownie, Carol, and I were not so local minded, and a guinea pig would be high on the list to skip. Carol and I would always try to find a place off the beaten path where the locals might be. We finally wandered into a restaurant that looked busy.

The hostess told us the dining room was full, with a rather long wait time. Seeing our disappointment, the hostess said that they had an overflow area upstairs, but it only had room for one communal table that held about ten or twelve guests. "Great! We'll take it," we all said together. The stairway was very narrow and steep, no handrails or OSHA sign of approval; the room was small and dimly lit and the old wood table was soon surrounded by other diners of other English-speaking tourists.

While waiting for our drinks, Brownie spoke up, "Hello everyone … we are from the States and my name is Brownie Flanders." And then Susan said, "Hi, I'm Susan, Brownie's wife." Then Carol and I introduced ourselves and said that we were from Michigan. At the end of the table, a lady named Cheryl said she was from California but grew up in Michigan. While sipping the local cordials and waiting for our dinners I asked the girl from California, "What part of Michigan were you from? Oh … a little town outside of Detroit, you wouldn't know it." "Really," I said, "I'm from a little town close to Detroit." She said she was from Wayne.

"Wayne!!!" I said excitedly. "Wayne … that's where I'm from. No way. Are you kidding me?" I asked if she went to Wayne High. She answered, "Yes, class of 1976."

"Carol and I were '62. Where did you live?" I asked. "Woodbrook Drive." I almost spit out my drink. "Woodbrook on the west side of town just north of Michigan Avenue?"

"Yes, that's it."

No way, now we are both getting a little excited, talking louder and the entire group joined in our mutual amazement. "Carol and I lived on Hubbard St., the first house from Michigan Avenue." Everyone's attention was focused on the coincidence. I asked who her neighbors were and then new exactly where she had lived. A short walk between us. She would have passed our house to get to hers. Wait … there's more.

Everyone settled down and we were all talking amongst ourselves about how strange it was. One in a million, I guess. Then I began to tell her that we now lived in Charlevoix and Florida and that we had owned Parkway Office Supply on Wayne Rd in Westland.

She jumped up from her chair, knocking it over with a scream. "I thought your name sounded familiar!" "Oh, do you know the store?" Now she was laughing and smiling and really excited. Yelling. "Mr. Hisey! I used to work for you as a co-op student during my senior year!" Unbelievable. Now that's a small world.

The night flight back to Lima is worth mentioning. It was extraordinarily magical and beautiful as the pilot weaved between gods billowing clouds lit from the bright full moon above and winks of lightning below and around us as the fragile tubed plane of metal and fasteners bounced and swayed above the jagged peaks of the Andes. We are all so small, so insignificant. Just wandering in our own ways through a path of brief moments. Through fate or luck or happenstance I have found moments of clarity when my God has opened nature's curtain for a glimpse of enlightenment. Standing tall, alone, grinning, thinking, thanking, on top of a ski mountain in a screaming blizzard or diving serenely into a tunnel of brilliant coral and fish. Or jumping into a pristine bottomless glacier lake or getting a wink from a lightning strike below, while flying high above the Andes. Hallelujah.

* * *

In August, Bob Bytwerk, who had bought our old house on Thistle Downs a few years earlier, (not from us) and kept his boat on the other side of our shared dock on Round Lake. He asked Tracy Sell if he knew anyone who could help him drive his boat up to the North Channel in Canada. Apparently, Tracy said, "Yes, your boat neighbor Jon." So, he did and soon after I was unpacking my gear inside a tiny aft captain's quarters on Bob's boat—a European modern style 52' yacht. By the time we shoved off there were seven souls on board, plus a dog!

There are two memorable episodes about this trip. First, at Lake Topaz, Bob was struggling walking up the strenuous trail and was helped by a Canadian park ranger who happened to be there with an all-terrain vehicle and gave him a ride. Bob was in his early 80s and suffered from hip and knee problems. Finally, at the lake I gave my normal intel talk to everyone about the secluded lake's history and the two traditional places to jump safely into the clear cold Topaz. One about five or six feet high and the other over 30.

Joking, I said to Bob, thinking he may attempt to jump standing close to the kiddie rock, "I'll jump in if you do." "Heck no, I'm jumping off the high one, and if I do it, you have to. I dare you." "Oh crap ..." I whispered. The last time I was here, my acrophobia was troublesome. Now it was much worse. I swore then I would never jump from the high cliff again.

Bob struggled, sometimes crawling, barely able to reach the top, and when he did, he didn't even pause. He just jumped, no thinking and no fanfare or stage show. When he was swimming back to shore, he yelled, "Your turn Jon!" with a big smile. Reluctantly, slowly, I climbed to the top, hoping for a twisted ankle or a snake bite. I was scared and nervous standing on the edge, looking down, looking around, looking at everyone looking at me. Crap ... I plugged my nose, said my prayer, and took my last and final high ledge jump into the incomparable pristine Topaz. Thank you, Bob.

Second, the return voyage of the trip started mid-morning from Gore Bay Marina in the middle of the north side of Manitoulin Island. The boat's cruising speed in moderate conditions was close to 30 miles per hour. Pretty good for a boat that size. We stopped in Detour to fill our diesel tanks, and to check in with US customs via the dock master's telephone at the shore office. While walking back from the office toward the boat, I saw three armed custom agents talking to Bob while he was waving me to hurry. After answering all the questions and searching the yacht thoroughly for about two hours we were cleared to go.

Unfortunately, the wind had begun to kick up a bit which started a conversation to either continue to Charlevoix or to stop at Mackinaw to spend the night and wait for the forecasted wind speed to settle down. They expressed their desire to go for Charlevoix. Bob and crew left the ultimate decision with me. A few miles before Mackinaw City, Grant (Bob's son-in-law) came up to the top deck helm station, from where I had steered the entire seven-day cruise. Grant told me that he and Bob had been closely monitoring the weather, and that the wind was going to top out at 12- to 15-mph out of the northwest, and wave height would be up to three feet until diminishing in the early evening. That moderate forecast combined with the boat's size and speed suggested that we sail on to Charlevoix.

The Straits of Mackinac are notorious for unexpected, quick bouts of temper. Experienced Michigan boaters know not to mess around with the Straits.

Here we go! Just a few miles west of the bridge the wind started making its noise, and soon the waves were breaking well over the forecasted three feet. Grant came up and took the wheel momentarily while I scurried down for my foul weather rain gear. It wasn't long before six- to eight-foot waves began to crash over the starboard bow and its water blown to the upper helm station, tossing my rain hat into the lake. And it didn't take long after that for the storm to increase its wind and wave spray, flexing its muscle to remind everyone who the boss was.

My eyes were fixated on the abandoned lighthouse in the

distance, fighting the wheel to keep it on my port side. Grant came up to the top of the ladder and shouted, "Are you all right Jon? Do you want to use the cabin's helm?" Yes!" and "No!" without turning around to see him retreat to the safety of the warm dry main salon to watch from there. The Bimini top had folded itself back, I was soaking wet, every piece of clothing was wet. My rain gear was useless, no match for the strong wind and heavy surf. My need to relieve myself became so great, I just stood there steering with both hands, fighting the push of the wind and to keep the approaching lighthouse to my port. I peed my pants. It didn't matter, it just "flushed out" with rain and lake water.

I made a terrible beginner's sailing mistake by focusing all my attention on the imaginary straight line from the bow to the old lighthouse. I didn't notice the amount of southerly drift the strong wind had moved us. Luckily, I happened to steal a glance at the depth finder to see 12 feet blink on its screen. The boat drew close to four feet of draft, the waves were six to seven feet, and the boulders could be anywhere from three to ten feet. Do the math. I was in shock! I had put myself into the crosshairs of calamity, and Bob and his family that had put their trust in me. Then the screen started to flash 10 feet and 12 feet erratically. I've snorkeled these waters many times through the years and have seen boulders bigger than school busses, even bigger than schools all around this area.

Instantly, I turned the wheel hard to starboard and headed straight north - northwest into the teeth of the storm, staring at the depth gauge, while riding the huge waves up then crashing down with a frightful boom, swamping the bow, as it burrowed into the wall of the next wave, fighting every inch of the way. Finally, slowly, inexorably, the water depth began to steady at 12, then 14, then 15, back to 10 to 12 then go deep to 20 before I could breathe again at a steady 30 to 40 feet. In due course I made a careful, hard 90-degree turn south and safely passed the old lighthouse on our port side. We eventually arrived at the Charlevoix channel for the 8:00 bridge in calm and quiet seas. I can't imagine what they were thinking down below, but I do know they were hanging on to something.

That was luck. I think that I came very, very close to a fatal accident that was my fault. My nightmares persisted for several months; remnants of the boat being blown about while people in the water were being smashed against the shores, rocks, and the little dog staring at me with — what the hell just happened eyes — while somehow riding the waves on a broken table. I've been beaten and bruised by all the Great Lakes except Lake Superior, but if you include an autumn skinny dip for a quick morning bath from its north Canadian shore, you can include Superior too.

You have to respect the Great Lakes before you can love them. I love the Great Lakes.

*　*　*

Carol and I began to close out our travels of 2011 on December 16 when we flew to Budapest, Hungary, and began our 12-day Christmas Danube River cruise from Budapest. It ended in Nuremberg, Germany, where we sat in the spectator's balcony in the courtroom where twenty-four surviving Nazi leaders were tried and convicted by an international military tribunal for crimes against humanity in 1946. The world's first.

River cruising is an easy way to see the historical highlights, castles, small villages, and large cities of importance along critical European rivers, but I suggest you wait until you are old. Until then rent a car and get yourself a paper map and a new pair of walking shoes.

On March 2, 2012, Carol's Dad, J.D. Clark, passed away at age

96 in East Lansing, Michigan, with Carol, her sisters, and Joan by his side. If there is a gate to heaven, J.D. Clark went through it.

That summer we closed on the sale of the Parkway Office Supply real estate, marking another end of an important chapter of my life and family's. Jon and his wife, Regina, chose to make Parkway a career, but the big box stores changed everything, and they had eventually sold the business side of Parkway a few years earlier. The office supply business was our family's benefactor for over 40 years. Its early success was ensured by the help of Carol and dedicated long-time employees. They included Cindy, Joyce, Ross and especially Carolyn Golemo. Daughter Joan, throughout her school years and son Jon from the beginning when he helped pack up the station wagon with our $500 starting inventory. Within its first ten years gross sales went from $0 to over $1.1 million. That success gave me the freedom and allowed me to devote time and attention to J.A.H. Development, plus several other businesses and partnerships of varying sizes and importance.

I used to say, "It's great being self-employed, as long as you have a good boss." I wasn't just attempting to give myself an often-undeserved pat on the back, but to say that you have to think more and work more and know more to get the respect of your employees, customers, and vendors. That logic applies the same as selling a $2.00 pack of pencils to a $500,000 condominium.

In the morning of June 5, 2012, our good friend and neighbor Ron Taht died in Cape Coral, Florida. I still think of Ron while fishing in Pine Island Sound or using the tools he left me, or his shirt that I'm wearing now while writing.

Later In August our growing family started to gather in Charlevoix to celebrate our 50th wedding anniversary. I borrowed Don Jesmore's ski boat for a few days, and son-in-laws, Dave and Todd, helped me launch *Goofy,* the hydroplane I had built in the late '90s. On the 16th, the whole family went to Mackinac Island and did the usual—rented bikes, rode around the Island, took a carriage ride, enjoyed some food and fudge, and smelled the fresh horse manure. You can't beat that for such a special anniversary. The next day the children arranged a scavenger hunt through Charlevoix, and at about 5:30 in the afternoon we were surprised when a big black limousine arrived at the Cottage. All of the grandchildren joined Carol and me for a circuitous fun ride to the Weathervane for a steak and lobster dinner. Quite a change from the few that gathered at the Howard Johnson's in Belleville next to the 1-94 expressway fifty years ago for an impromptu dinner of the day's special hot turkey, mashed potatoes, and gravy for $2.95 per before leaving on our honeymoon.

On August 25, astronaut hero Neil Armstrong died, at 82 years old. His funerary urn was buried at sea. The ceremony was witnessed by his family and an honor guard, on a US Navy cruiser. Taps were played while the small crowd saw the small splash of a huge event and watched the nation's hero disappear somewhere off the coast of Florida. A life's journey that soared to and from the moon to a nest somewhere in the deep Atlantic Ocean.

*   *   *

We finished the year of travel by flying from Chicago to Venice, Italy, for a grand tour. Upon arrival we took a water taxi to the Hotel Boscolo Venezia. It was very nice, very comfortable. Sleep came quickly while planning our next day of wandering the city on our own before meeting the tour group. Unfortunately, it was too comfortable. We slept over 16 hours uninterrupted before a curious maid woke us up.

We rushed, afraid to be late for our scheduled 4:00 p.m. meeting, throwing everything in our suitcases before waving down a water taxi for the 20-minute ride to Italy's mainland. Our trip included Venice, Florence, Pisa, Rome, and the Sistine Chapel and Vatican, where we casually gawked at the glass enclosed bodies of legendary Pope John XXIII and recently canonized St. John Paul II and others. We walked the ruins of Pompeii, Sorrento, Isle of Capri, and the beautiful Amalfi Coast before flying from Naples back to Chicago. In my view, Italy is beyond comparison of cultural history and natural beauty.

In the spring of 2013, we drove to Joan's for a night before starting our Amtrak train adventure from Kalamazoo to San Francisco. We lingered the days away from the train's vista windows—fixated by the rhythm of the train's wheels on the tracks and the scenery passing by; from overgrown back yards and old unkempt homes with broken back doors and rusted derelict cars of the cities' abandoned neighborhoods; through the miles and miles of corn and cows; to the peaks of the Rocky Mountains. Evenings were spent in the dining car with strangers and sharing the "boxed wine." It's a very beautiful country and we are lucky to be in it, and I am grateful to have visited all fifty states.

A car was rented in San Francisco for a leisurely motor trip to Portland, Oregon. We "saddled" the San Andreas fault (I swear I felt the Pacific plate move away from the North American plate). We walked among the mighty redwoods and drove our rent-a-car through a giant Redwood tree near Leggett, California, with two inches to spare and swam a brief moment in the cold surf of the mighty Pacific. After two nights in Portland a short commuter shuttle train took us to Seattle before transferring to our train's sleeper car back to Kalamazoo.

That fall, we flew to Athens, Greece, and took a twelve-stop local bus to the port of Piraeus and our hotel for a night before starting our 16-day cruise on Holland America's Rotterdam, a 1200 plus passenger ship. It included the Greek Islands of Mykonos, Santorini, Lesbos, Corfu, and Rhodes. We cruised north, passing the infamous historically significant shores of

Britain's World War I disastrous Gallipoli. Then through the Dardanelles Strait, which separates Europe on the west and Asia to the east, before stopping at Istanbul, Turkey, for two nights. We spent time in the famous Blue Mosque and the Hagia Sophia and toured the city's largest 1500-year-old water cistern. All the popular sights were explored before continuing down to Ephesus on the Asian side. We visited the final home of the Mother Mary and drank from the ever-flowing spring that was near her house, before returning to Athens.

*   *   *

Carol and I decided to revisit the British Virgin Islands in the spring 2014 and invited Clarke and Claire (our two available grandchildren) to join us. We boarded the last day's ferry, *Bomba Charger* (our favorite way to travel between the USA and BVI's), in St. Thomas, USVI to Roadtown, Tortola. We spent the night at our favorite hotel, Treasure Isle, that soon lost its luster when there was no hot water, and the pool was closed. "Hey kids, it's a tropical island." The hotel was located close to town and convenient for shopping for a week's supply of provisions. We rented a sailboat from the Moorings and sailed to the places and anchorages that we loved, including the Baths on Virgin Gorda and snorkeling the wreck of the Rhone. It was all good, but the town had changed. The locals seemed rushed, and looked at their sandals while walking without smiling, their faces looked worried. They wore watches. I blame the big cruise ships that started unloading naive innocents for a few hours with their new shoes, oversized sunglasses and fancy tote bags with several kinds of suntan lotion looking for shade in a USA pub chain to drink their watered-down rum and cokes and Budweisers. They cheapened the authenticity of a once idyllic British Caribbean Island.

They wore watches.

The following little anecdote survived the delete cut of several dozen small paragraphs of trivial trips of travel or facts of one-time importance. In July I flew solo to Utah to pick up ten-year-old granddaughter Jenevieve. After a few days in Park City we finally arrived back, delayed and late to the Traverse City airport. I clearly remember telling Jenevieve not to fall asleep and keep me awake. When we drove into Charlevoix and came to the top of the hill on Bridge St. and looked down at our beautiful tree-lighted city, Jenevieve said to me, "Grandpa … Charlevoix is in my destiny." It's funny what you remember. The treasures of a grandchild far outweigh a chest of gold and jewelry. A week later we drove to Pellston to pick up her mom and Charlie.

*　*　*

In September of 2014, the siren call of travel once again lured us to unseen places and cultures when we flew to Kirkenes, Norway, on four different airplanes to begin our seven-day cruise on the working cargo/ferry ship Hurtigruten. We sailed north past a sign embedded into a close-by shoreline rock that marked the Arctic Circle and gulped the traditional spoon of cod liver oil. We spent the days stopping in remote little villages and watched them load and unload fish, cars, and people. One memorable fjord was so narrow they warned us not to touch the rock walls on either side of the ship. They were not kidding. Our voyage ended in Bergen. A very interesting trip, another one of our many favorites.

From Bergen we flew to St. Petersburg, Russia, to start our 14-day, 400-plus-mile Volga River cruise to Moscow. We enjoyed the leisurely pace and many ports-of-call in cities and hamlets that seemed to be stuck in the last century of Russia's rural isolated back country. These forsaken little towns along the Volga River suffered horrifically during and after the Russian Bolshevik revolution in the 1919–1922 transformation to oppressive communism. Communism was supposed to be the panacea of the working man. It was not.

On our last day of touring Moscow, while standing in the middle of Red Square, I asked our guide if we could separate from the group and stay a little longer to see the over 90-year-old embalmed corpse of Russia's first communist party chairman, Vladimir Lenin, in his infamous tomb in Red Square. I remember learning of this in the seventh grade. She hesitated a moment before answering, "Yes, I guess so. No one has ever asked me that before." She looked at her watch and said, "But you don't have much time. You have to be back to your boat no later than 5:00 p.m. Your ship is moving to a different port. Don't forget 5:00 p.m. Your ship will leave without you." She then pointed us in the direction of the entrance to the subway and told us to be sure to get off at a certain stop. Carol and I looked at each other as we saw the tour bus slowly leave the corner stop with our fellow passengers as they started back to the safety of our boat. I told our guide that I was a little concerned because there were no English signs or English-speaking people anywhere. She said, "Don't worry, there are English subtitles in most of the signs throughout Russia. She gave explicit instructions to get off at the ninth stop. "Whatever you do—get off at the ninth stop." Carol and I hurried through Lenin's tomb. He looked small, weak, and frail, and his face was a ghostly powder white. Of course he did. He had been lying there for almost 100 years. Dead at 53 years old in 1924. How could a man look so sickly unimportant and be so horribly significant in the modern world's history?

We quick walked to the close by subway station and gave the ticket person a slip of paper that our guide gave us as well as some of our rubles to the agent. We then took what seemed to be a quarter mile deep escalator down to the tracks. We got on the train, hoping it was the right one. At the first stop I held out my fisted hand and unfolded a finger down while Carol and I said, "one," out loud. We repeated the routine with my fingers and counting out loud each stop until the train started to slow for the ninth stop. "Nine," I said rather loudly as we prepared to stand and heard several of our fellow Russian passengers say in unison with smiles "dyev-yat!" or nine. We walked up a few steps to daylight and had no idea where we were. Now what?

The guide said we would be able to see the boat from the subway station. Well, she was wrong; we could not see anything, and no signs were in English. It was a little after 4:30 in the afternoon when a nicely dressed middle aged Russian man approached us and asked in perfect English "May I help you?" "Yes, we are lost." He told us we were in the right spot. The Viking boat was hidden behind the trees in the park across the boulevard and it was about a 10 or 15 minute walk. We were the last ones on the boat and watched the waiting crew hoist up the gangway immediately after we stepped onto the boat's deck. That was close. That was stressful. That was luck. Was seeing the dead Lenin laid out in his elaborate tomb worth it? No! They should burn him up and throw his ashes into the city dump. I have come to believe after all our travels that the citizenry of the world would get along just fine without ill-begotten politicians.

We ended the year with a Christmas cruise to Mexico and a stop in Cozumel and a ferry boat to the Yucatan Peninsula where I cave dived a few years earlier. We were bussed inland to the Mayan Temple Coba, the tallest structure in northern Yucatan, and climbed the 130 steps to the top of the pyramid. Carol and I rested next to a slab of stone where hundreds of years ago they sacrificed animals and innocent virgins to their god of harvest. I wondered what the parents were thinking when they walked their beautiful young daughter to her death. Did they cover their eyes or cry when the high priestess cut open her beating breasts and pulled her heart out to the cheers of the crowd? The evolution of cultures, customs and the past and current religions of various degrees of sophistication have interested me my entire life.

On the drive back to Cape Coral we stopped to see, for the first and probably last time, the grave of my grandfather Ventry Ross Hisey and his wife, Henrietta. They were buried in Miami Memorial Park Cemetery. It is a huge cemetery with a big arched entrance, so I stopped and went into the office to introduce myself and to get directions to the graves. They gave me a nice fold-out map with some verbal instructions. We hopped back in the car, buckled up, and started. We drove about 200 feet to the first corner and looked at each other then looked at the map again and looked back at the office just behind us, we got out of the car, walked a dozen steps and there they were.

*   *   *

Our drive north to Charlevoix that year included our first leg of the Lincoln Highway motor trip from Florida to Times Square, New York City. The highway ends in San Francisco's Lincoln Park, with South Bend, Indiana, as an intermediate destination. A few of the significant stops along the way included Princeton, and the home of Einstein; the Edison Laboratories; and Gettysburg, Pennsylvania (I was previously there with Tim Dyer and Bill Coole in late 1961). We toured some of the war's bloodiest battlefields that eventually ended the Civil War in the north's favor. And walked through President Eisenhower's home where his golf clubs still waited by the doorway to the garage. One night we stayed in the 250-year-old (1757) Fairfield Inn where President John Adams frequented just outside of Gettysburg where we ate our breakfast at the same table that Ike and Mamie often dined. We then drove to the Shanksville 2001 memorial site, and a lengthy detour took us to Frank Lloyd Wright's famous architectural gem, Fallingwater.

We drove true, driving the actual Lincoln Highway by our extensive guidebooks. We stayed in old mom and pop motels and outdated, almost empty city hotels and ate in old diners and pubs that reeked of history, never staying or eating at a national chain. We arrived in Charlevoix on May 31, having covered 2,710 miles.

*   *   *

Our roam of the globe for 2015 was a 26-day marathon trip that took us to the Republic of Ireland and into the troubled Northern Ireland. Luckily it was during an unusually peaceful period between the Catholics and Protestants. For me it was especially interesting to walk the Belfast shipyard that built the doomed *Titanic* (I had been a member of the Titanic Historical Society for several years). From Ireland we spent over a week in delightful Scotland with its castles, and the environs of King Arthur and on the waters of Loch Ness where we searched for its fabled monster.

Our next country was the island nation of Iceland. A geological wonder world of hot geothermal baths and blue lagoons. There were waterfalls and a trench that you can walk in and put one hand on the North American continent and the other hand on the European. That was special. The whole world is special. See it if you can. While reviewing Carol's journals and sorting photographs from around the world I was reminded and amazed of our fortunate travel experiences. When mentioning to Carol of all our fateful and lucky travel, she thought obsession was more like it.

*   *   *

In the fall of 2016, we again found ourselves in San Diego, California, to start our 48-day cruise on Holland America's *Veendam*, a sister ship to the *Zaandam* — another mid-size boat with a capacity of about 1250 passengers. We crossed the Pacific Ocean to Australia and Auckland, New Zealand, with stops to explore, swim, and tour in Hawaii, Fiji, Tasmania, and many other small Pacific islands. I loved the routine of life on a boat in the middle of deep, very deep water. From Auckland we flew back to Brisbane, Australia, and shared a six-person, five-hour drive north to Cairns to snorkel the Great Barrier Reef. A must see for me and an important piece of our trip.

Unfortunately, the boat ride out to the 130,000-square-mile reef, one of the Seven Wonders of the World, was more enjoyable than the reef. Snorkeling was sad. A majority of the reef's coral was bleached out and dying. It was disheartening to see a once-thriving underwater ecosystem passing away just a few inches from our dive masks. Climate change had ravaged the reefs with rising water temperatures that killed 90% of it. Shameful. In our time, climate change deniers were still among us, even in high levels of influence and government officials, including our newly elected president by the Electoral College (not the popular vote). I would hope that they could see for themselves firsthand the harm that fossil fuels have caused. But they won't, or can't, and even if they could, they would probably blame it on octopus poop or another ridiculous opinion that was fostered on social media or a certain TV network.

Abraham Lincoln famously said, "You can fool some of the people some of the time, but you can't fool all of the people all of the time." I hope to God he's right.

Stubbornness leads to arrogance, and arrogance leads to ignorance. —JAH

After two days of exploring around Cairn we took a small plane to see the famous ancient Ayers Rock for a few nights. It is an oasis in the middle of Australia, a huge stand-alone rock that ascends out of nowhere in the middle of the vast, remote desert. It is a mystical and spiritual stone called Uluru by the indigenous people. We were lucky to witness (with a glass of champagne) a rare super moon rise over the massive 500-million-year-old sandstone monolith. Another once in a lifetime opportunity to witness one of the worlds many wonders.

* * *

I vividly remember March 10, 2017, because that evening I sat next to *Apollo 15* Command Module Pilot, astronaut Al Worden. We were at a nice upscale restaurant in Ft. Myers, Florida, with friends Janna Winn, and Marsie and Roger Gowdy. He was very friendly and gracious, especially after his second vodka martini.

He was my new best friend. Al had family ties in East Jordan and had eaten several times at the Weathervane. Janna told him I owned it and that I had developed the Edgewater Inn. I flattered him by expressing how much I enjoyed reading his signed first edition autobiography, *Falling to Earth*. He asked how much I paid for it. Odd.

Later in the evening I told Al about my press credentials and being the closest person to witness the launch of *Apollo 11,* by stepping into the shore's sand of the Banana River. He didn't appear to be very impressed when he said, "Hell Jon, if you think that's close you should try sitting on top of the damn rocket during liftoff!" Some people are hard to impress.

For several years Carol and I were hosts to the winter season's end with a large Kentucky Derby horse race party at our Florida home. Usually there would be about 20 guests with lots of pot-luck food and southern style Mint Juleps, some games, and lottery style horse betting. I would often mix up prize money every year for different finishes, such as $20 win for a horse in 5th place, and $10 for 3rd place, and $0 for 4th, etc. But the one everyone seemed to get excited about was the D.A.L. winner with an abundance of hype and a wrapped secret prize of little value for the horse who happened to finish "Dead Ass Last."

2017's Kentucky Derby party was unique in view of the fact that Janna brought "my new friend," astronaut Al Worden. He definitely added additional excitement to the party. He talked to everyone, posed for photos, and was the center of attention, especially after his horse came in 4th place. He just could not understand how my prize money was distributed. "What kind of an operation are you running here Jon?" Of course nobody could understand; I couldn't understand it, that is the joke. Al and I milked it together, laughing all the way. After the race a few of us told a joke or two and Al maybe 3 or 4, 5 or 6. Our neighbor Lynn did her Swedish joke, and then I started by telling a joke that most friends had already heard, (some more than once). After their moans of "No Jon, not that one again," I proceeded. "Why do they only put 239 beans in a can of bean soup?" Al joined in reply, "I don't know Jon, why do they only put 239 beans in a can of bean soup?" The fake anticipation was dramatic … "because if they added one more bean it would be (now several joined me in the punch line … two fouarty!" An evening's memory that still burns bright. Al and Janna broke up a few months later. Sadly, Al died March 18, 2020.

* * *

Our 2018 journey back to South America was especially memorable when we flew from Ft. Myers to Buenos Aires, Argentina, to board the Holland American ship *Zaandam* with about 1,200 other passengers for a cruise to Antarctica with stops at Uruguay and the Falkland Islands. We crossed the tempestuous Drake Passage to the waters of Antarctica's Peninsula and the Weddell Sea. For five days Carol and I had the privilege of the few who have had the unique opportunity to slowly and cautiously explore by sea the unparalleled stark beauty of the frozen subcontinent. Antarctica was cold, no surprise. It was eerie, serene, and had a peculiar quietness. No sounds of life. No trees or natures green. During the night the ship was in idle or very slow moving. Sometimes you could hear the continent's ice screech, like it was in pain, and sometimes you could hear the splash of an iceberg calving. The captain carefully and slowly maneuvered through fields of icebergs. Shaped by nature, some looked like simple boxes of random sizes just aimlessly floating in the sea and some were hills like sleeping white elephants. Each of them seemed unique and distorted from wind and magic. Truly natures beauty at it's finest.

Returning north, sailing back again through the turbulent (very rough) waters of Drake Passage and into Chile's calm Straits of Magellan; a winding route of lakes and channels that link the Pacific and Atlantic oceans. We spent the night in the northern port of Punta Arenas. In the morning a small plane took some of us to Patagonia to get our passport stamped and spent the day bus touring its remote unique and impressive grandeur before cruising north to Santiago, Chile. We were grateful for the experience.

In February 2018 we bought Lot 21 on Lake Michigan, 4245 Lake Shore Drive, in Clipperview, south of Charlevoix for $110,000. In May, construction started on our new house that I designed. We named it Lake House III (1st Lake House 1974, 2nd Lake House 1980). We spent our first night in our new home on New Year's Eve 2018, before driving down to Cape Coral for the winter.

If you are lucky enough to live on the shores of Lake Michigan . . . you are lucky enough.
—JAH

* * *

In 2020 the world population was approaching 8 billion and the United States was nearing 340,000,000. The new decade also brought with it the new Coronavirus plague and the November presidential election. Fear ruled the world. The world stood still. Corona confusion dominated the news, conspiracies, misinformation, and civil unrest percolated to the forefront of an already over-stoked citizenship. Political leadership failed to coalesce a united population to conquer the world's deadly dilemma.

And to pour fuel on an already confused and divisive citizenry, the defeated past president willfully and tragically decided not to concede his loss, and did not attend the inauguration of President Biden, but instead chose to lie. I cannot think of a more selfish and harmful act he inflicted upon the disunited United States of America. All he had to do for his country, for its citizenry, and to the benefit of our standing in the world, is simply say "I lost." A lie without end. A close shot in the heart of our already wounded democracy. How can a man that was born into wealth and privilege be so cynical and be so willing to inflict so much damage to our nation's soul and democracy and its institutions. Another moment in our young country's history that will be taught in school rooms for centuries.

* * *

In the midst of speculation and concern of the pandemic, I invited son Jon and grand boys, Jon Andrew, Clarke, and Charles to an eight-day, 250-mile Colorado River rafting expedition through the Grand Canyon. Our boatman, Bobby Skinner, was a veteran of over 300 trips. The best guide on the river. He regaled our small group with stories and taught us about the canyon's millions-year-old geological strata. Another one of the seven Wonders of the World that I was lucky to visit. Camping nightly, deep into the canyon along the swift river's edge, on a cot without a tent, under millions of stars, was unforgettable and, I expect it could be, the last of my life's memorable adventures. The best, made better by sharing it with "my boys." I hope it will be their touchstone of travel and that my "girls" also enjoy a life of curiosity and be enlightened and enriched by their journeys, opened to the diversity of the worlds people and their customs and culture without judgment.

The river's violent rapids and the river's peaceful drifts again gave me the sense of peace, irrelevance and insignificance within the scope of nature's mysteries and the infinity of dark space. I'm grateful for the view from the top of mountains and lucky enough to explore the bottoms of rivers, lakes, seas and oceans, but nothing knocked me back and put me in my place than the eight days of rafting on the Colorado River through the grandest canyon of the world.

*　*　*

So … in the end, when I am called to the podium to accept my award for an extraordinary life, I would first want to thank the supremacy of the universe and the spark of life. I also would like to reach back with gratitude to my parents and ancestors of the millennia for good health and the traits of work, empathy, ingenuity, curiosity, and common sense.

It goes without saying that I am grateful for my wife, Carol, and children, Joan, Jon, Jenifer, and Jessica and our grandchildren for their love and unique enhancements to my odyssey.

And, lastly before the music starts and the director of this show waves me off with the hook in his hand, I can't leave without mentioning Tim, Barbara, Grant, Jack, Dick, Leon, and the hundreds of friends and positive acquaintances, both men and women. And of course, fate and luck.

Maybe I'll hear the start of the rockets roar. Maybe I will be lucky enough that it will awaken me for a final glimpse of life's light, or of death's enlightenment. Maybe I will be waved on by Mom or Dad, maybe I will see Jesus or Confucius, a righteous Pope, a prophet or a minister, Buddha, or my childhood dog Rusty. Maybe God almighty. Maybe. Maybe not.

"Who's To Know?"

ADDENDUMS

In the early afternoon on the last day of the Grand Canyon expedition during a slow drift, our boatman Bobby Stringer made a farewell "speech." He thanked us for coming and appreciated our spirit of adventure. He said that our group did it all! We all shouted with echoes from the canyon Hip-Hip Hooray, Hip-Hip Hooray, Hip-Hip Hooray, and then Bobby read the Boatman's Prayer before motoring a few miles for our disembarkment.

Our raft on the Grand Canyon Rapids: Clarke, Jon Andrew, and Charles are on the bow and Jon C. and I near the stern.

BOATMAN'S PRAYER

May your journey be long, and the river of your journey
carry you well.
May the rapids that lay ahead be powerful and treacherous
and the route through prove difficult and rewarding.
May you find the serenity of the calm water.
May you lay some night on the hard ground so you will not sleep
and might notice the heavens.
May the morning reward you.
And may you greet that morning as if you are newly born.
May you know death, so when she comes you may greet her
with dignity.
May your days gather behind you like stories and spread out
before you like a dream at the end of each day.
May you know that you have left little trace and may
your feet ache.
May you find solace and wisdom in the setting sun and in the
moment that it slips over the horizon may its mystery be
revealed, only as a mystery.
May you hear rhythm of love beat in your heart so that you
might sing to it and others sing along.
May your mind be set free and your body set in motion.
May your grandchildren kneel down at the bank of a stream
to gather pure clean water from it and may they give thanks
to you for the gift.

—Benjie

Joan C Hisey, 1980

MY CHILDHOOD MEMORIES of growing up start with our home on Hubbard St. in Wayne and our family's large Fourth of July parties in our backyard with its swimming pool. Swimming, jumping off a high platform that Dad built, and jumping and doing somersaults on our in-ground trampoline. Selling newspapers at the Wayne Bank.

Dad coming in every night to take our socks off, open the window, and kiss us good night on our forehead. Going too many times to Niagara Falls. "Never go to the grocery store hungry." I remember shopping with Dad and our cart would overflow with stuff Mom would never buy. Dad teaching me how to ski, "bend the knees." Skipping stones into Lake Michigan from the first Lake House. Mom rubbing my back when I was sick. Sailing to Cedar Point on our boat, *Paper Clipper* in ten-foot waves. Making popcorn for Dad for five cents and watching old movies with family. Mom and Dad watching me as a cheerleader at all of my home games. Jumping off boats for money that was never paid. Christmas Eve sleeping with Jen and Jessica while Dad made lots of Santa noises. Finding one hundred dollars in my Christmas book. Mom piercing my ears. Working behind the counter at Parkway Office Supply from 14 years old and up. Hundreds of skiing memories at Boyne Mountain, Boyne Highlands, and the Rocky Mountains out west. Learning to scuba dive in the British Virgin Islands. My Outward Bound adventure started with a twenty-hour bus ride from Detroit to Asheville, North Carolina, in the Blue Ridge Mountains, an experience that definitely impacted my life. Difficult challenges included a half marathon with backpack, rock climbing, rappelling, and white-water canoeing and a three-day lonesome solo somewhere within the Table Rock Mountains. I completed my challenges with thirty bee stings which would undoubtedly make it the hardest course of all my siblings.

WHEN I REFLECT ON MEMORIES of my childhood, I've always felt safe and loved and it was filled with plenty of adventures. I can remember as a young boy being dropped off by Dad and Uncle Jerry at the beginner's hill at Boyne Mountain and having lunch with them in the cafeteria and a few runs together after lunch. One time Dad and I were driving back to Canton and stopped at a little ski hill near Grayling. There was just an old rope tow and Dad

Jon C. Hisey, 1981

was trying to teach me how to get up the hill with this rope that was running through my hands and told me to slowly grip the rope. It was a struggle; my skis were going up and down the rope's trail as I hung on for dear life. I can still remember Dad shouting as I approached the top, "Come on Jon, you can do it, don't let go, you are almost there," he hollered, "you are almost there, DON'T LET GO!" That was the moment I was launched twenty or thirty feet into the air and almost completed three full somersaults before landing in a huge pile of snow on my back. When we moved into our first house on Hubbard Street they left a cat named Matilda and we all camped out in sleeping bags in front of the living room's fireplace. Hubbard Street was where I was introduced to home improvements. We often had large pool and trampoline parties. At the first Lake House Mom and I would take the yellow canoe and paddle out as far as we dared into Little Traverse Bay. Many fond memories of the Lake House, campfires, counting stars, being towed by Dad in the green van by skis or toboggan. Keeping warm by the fires in the Franklin stove. Selling *Dispatch* papers in the lobby of Wayne Bank and breaking up boxes as my first job at Parkway Office Supply. My first ski trip out west was to Steamboat Springs, Colorado, with Joan, Dad, and Uncle Jerry and skiing the last run down Heavenly Daze with Olympic winner Billy Kidd. Learning to sail with Dad on the Sunfish and *Paper Clipper*. Sailing to Cedar Point. Fearing death when caught in a terrible frightening storm on Lake Huron just past the Thunder Bay Lighthouse. Hundreds of ski runs with Dad, my favorite of them all, is when in the morning and the runs were groomed or had a light snow we would make figure eight tracks together. At eighteen I took a bus myself to Asheville, North Carolina, for my once-in-a-lifetime Outward Bound experience. Rappelling down Pickens Nose, backpacking every day, whitewater canoeing in the Chattooga River, where they filmed the movie, "Deliverance." It rained every day during my 3 days of solo. And I had to run a marathon through the mountains for my final. It taught me a lot about myself, and I vividly remember seeing my mother cry when she first saw my disheveled, dirty, worn-out body.

I FONDLY REMEMBER MY CHILDHOOD through the windows of our van or cars because it seemed like I was always on the move traveling back and forth between our home in Canton and our First Lake House in Charlevoix. Always stopping at Bill Knapps for the children's Giraffe meal and Dad coaxing me to order my hamburger and fries when I was four years old at McDonalds. Jessica and I on the YMCA stingray swim team. Sailing with Dad to Boblo Island amuse-

Jenifer A. Hisey, 1990

ment park in the Detroit River with cousin Janelle and Uncle Jerry and spending the night on *Paper Clipper*. Our dog Chester. Christmas morning and Dad blinding us with an extremely bright light video camera. Sitting on Dad's lap in the green van and pretending to drive and getting pulled over by a cop.

Sharing my bedroom with Grandma Beverly every summer. Dad chasing us around the house with a snapping towel. Running around the block with Dad before dinner. Counting pencils and erasers during Parkway's annual inventory. Playing catch with Dad with my new mitt. Jumping into Lake Michigan in front of the 2nd Lake House every time the Beaver Islander came by to catch waves. Seeing Michael Jackson concert at the Pontiac Silverdome. Climbing through the bathroom window at North Drive when we were all locked out to save the day. Making popcorn for Dad on movie nights for 25 cents. Going on ski trips out west and Dad's rule … I could pack anything I wanted as long as I could carry it. So, I stuffed my bag so much that I had to drag it to the car. Following Dad down my favorite ski runs at Beaver Creek, Centennial, Latigo, Tin Pants, and Gold Rush to the jump to "get big air" at the bottom. Cooking our own steaks over big flaming grates at Minturn Country Club between Vail and Beaver Creek and Dad almost burned the place down. My first trip to the North Channel on *Phase III,* on our 57' Chris-Craft boat.

Disney World. Living on *Phase III* for a summer. Construction cleaning at the Edgewater Inn. Dad's "Hambone" act. Whitefish dinners at the Weathervane. Sailing "Happy Heart" in the British Virgin Islands and snorkeling and anchoring out every night. Cutting down Christmas trees with a lot of character, usually on someone else's property. My Outward Bound adventure was to the Cascade Mountains in Oregon in the summer of 1990 (most difficult and expensive trip offered). One week of rafting on the Deschutes River, followed by three weeks of backpacking and mountaineering and three days of solo camp.

MY CHILDHOOD MEMORIES START at the first Lake House taking bike rides with Mom on the back of her bike. Swimming in the lake and picking raspberries next to the playground.

Jessica L. Hisey, 1992

Driving north from Canton to Charlevoix in the green van that had shag carpeting. Going to Niagara Falls. Hiking into woods, probably trespassing, to find our Christmas trees and Mom would bring hot dogs to roast and beans while Dad would try and talk like an Indian and tell Indian stories. Disney World and Space Mountain. YMCA swim team. Dad teaching me to ski at Boyne Highlands. Dad chasing me and Jen around in the North Drive house with a snapping towel, laughing, screaming, sometimes tearing up if we got smacked and Dad apologizing. Mammoth Cave. Sailing with Mom and Dad on *Paper Clipper*. Attending sailing camp at Culver Academy in Indiana where I raced Hobie Cats and one summer I taught sailing at the Belvedere Camp for children and would take them out on Lake Charlevoix and Round Lake by myself. Seeing Michael Jackson live in concert. Going to Washington, DC, and visiting the White House and memorials while Dad told us about the history. Train trip to New York City visiting Statue of Liberty, World Trade Centers, and lunch at The Fraunces Tavern where George Washington gave a farewell toast to his officers in the Continental Army. Dinner at the famous Tavern on the Green in Central Park and most of all sitting on the stage to see the musical, *Cats*. Numerous ski trips out west to Colorado and Utah.

Skiing with actor Tom Cruise in Beaver Creek where we had a condo. Bobsledding on Black Road behind Dad's truck. Making popcorn for Dad for 50 cents. Driving up north to Charlevoix with Dad in his Porche going 100 miles per hour. Traveling to the Virgin Islands when I was 13 years old. Learning to snorkel and seeing sharks, sea turtles, and thousands of fish, and Dad almost running into another boat while anchoring in the evening or leaving in the morning or both and Dad blaming it on a faulty transmission. One time in the North Channel on *Engenuity* we anchored at "The Pool" at the end of Baie of Finn and hiked up to Lake Topaz and jumped off a 100-foot cliff (Dad said thirty) and when I hit the water, I lost the top of my bathing suit. In 1990 when I was just 16 years old, I went to Outward Bound in Fresno, California. Twenty-three days of backpacking in the southern Sierra Mountains where I encountered rattlesnakes, grizzly bears, and other wildlife while learning survival skills. My backpack weighed forty-five pounds and usually hiked fifteen miles a day, sometimes on snow and ice and slept under a tarp in a snowstorm during my three solo days. I am grateful for the opportunity at such a young age and successfully completing the hardest Outward Bound experience of all.

The Grandchildren

Julia G Hisey

Jon A Hisey

Jenica R Hisey

Clarke D Stebbins

Claire J Stebbins

Jenevieve G Witham

Charles J Witham

Jaydee L Levy

A Gravesite Eulogy for
Beverly Grace Simpson Hisey

It's About Time.

HERE WE ARE, GATHERED THIS MORNING AROUND A SMALL GRAVE, marked with a little piece of granite among a vast field of thousands of other matriarchs, to say another goodbye, and to bury the cremains of our mom and grandmother, Beverly Grace Simpson Hisey.

We are all here because of her, most of us literally, with a portion of her DNA, or directly through family.

Some of us have vivid memories, we can still hear her voice: "The kitchen is closed!" Some have a resemblance or carry on traits, some habits, hopefully no one claims to have that distinct laughable laugh.

Lately, I have been thinking about, or asking myself, what would Mom say about the 14½ years it has taken her family to finally carry out her wish to place her remains in Acacia Memorial Cemetery, in Beverly Hills, Michigan, next to her mother and father. Maybe she would say, "Well … It's about time."

But she can't and she won't. There is no time in the eternity of heaven.

There can be no clocks, no sunrise or sunset. No lingering threat of mortality. Fourteen years is a mere fraction of a nanosecond in death. There is no time for Mom; her time has come and gone.

It is our time, it is our time to reflect, to thank her for our chance at life. A time to remember Mom as she was and now is, a spirit from the ages of our ancestry. And to consider our place within the continuing family of untold ancestors and future descendants.

It is our time to remember Mom as a person.

She was born Vera Paskevich, whose parents had fled Russia/ Hungary. Her father served in World War I. Little is known about him other than a factory worker at Ford's within a simple life of labor. Very little is known of her mother. We suspect her mother could have died in 1921 or '22 when she and a brother were given up for adoption. A lucky toddler when rescued from the Wayne County Social Services by Arthur and Augusta Simpson, the folks that she will be resting beside. Mom was raised in an upper middle-class lifestyle, at 16529 Westmoreland in Rosedale Park, an upscale neighborhood of Detroit. She became a talented pianist and performed in several concerts and ended her high school days with a debutante's ball at Redford's Country Club. After graduating from Michigan State, she married her college sweetheart, our father, James H. Hisey, and settled into the small town of Wayne, Michigan, where Mom enjoyed the company of influential friends with an active social life. A stay-at-home mother with three young boys ages about 1½ to 7 years old when divorce hit, and hit hard. Can we even imagine that?

She carried on, sometimes working two jobs, one in the day and, for a while, nights waiting tables for tips, occasionally serving guests that only a few short years before were her social peers. She would come home at night, and put the tip money in an envelope marked "special," maybe use it to take us to a circus or Tigers game or to spend a day at Boblo Island, or maybe help expenses with the road trip, just the four of us, to Florida in 1958. She was peerless to us.

It's time to honor our mother for the way she lived. Not as a saint, but with sacrifice, dignity, patience, generosity, and a selfless unspoken love. She chose kindness to all who crossed her path. She was grateful, enjoyed a good laugh (remember the laugh), enjoying it even more if it was about her, the center of attention (some of us have that trait now). She had hundreds of longtime friends. When she was dying we received well over 100 cards, notes, and phone calls.

She never complained, she was always benevolent, never malicious, and often taken for granted. Mom rarely if ever showed a tear. Even during the last few weeks of her life, after her diagnosis became terminal, there was never a sigh of why me, or self-pity. I never saw a tear, not once, not one. Mom always did the best she could, and her best was always good enough, very good enough.

It is time now to inter her remains to conclude this chapter of our lives.

Some, probably most of us, will never return here again. In a few years her memory will fade like an old photograph, or occasionally reappear when finding a penny on the sidewalk, and eventually in a few generations, all will be forgotten. So, let's take time to reflect on our unique and special mother and to ponder each of our own short lives in this constant rhythm of beginnings and endings.

Because, after all, after love … after everything else … "It's About Time."

God Bless the Soul of our mother and grandmother.

—Jon A. Hisey

NIGHT SAIL

A Short Story by Jon A. Hisey

THE SUN HAD ALREADY QUIT FOR THE DAY, leaving palettes of remnants of oranges, pinks, and lavender brushstrokes. You could still see the leeward leaning birches, maple and cedar trees on shore real good. Most were already beginning to shed their fall colors, as Tommy and his father rounded up at Harbor Point and began to set their new heading. The air still had a breath of heat and had pretty well winded itself out, but the father still put a wrap on the starboard winch and cleated the line tight, then coiled the excess carefully, making loops between his elbow and palm. Tommy watched him work, grinning a glimpse of contentment.

The man and the boy made their way slowly along the north side of Little Traverse Bay. Some of the big homes had already begun to cover their windows with big sheets of painted wood, and they could see other pieces leaning against front steps and colonnades. They saw distant headlights moving along Highway 31 between Charlevoix and Petoskey. Tommy sat next to his dad. It was a small fiberglass sailboat with a small cabin, and a small refrigerator and a two-burner stove top. A compact two-person bunk in the bow and a berth portside. They were alone on the water except for some resting gulls and salmon fisherman scattered along the south's drop-off, trolling the bottom of the deep limestone ledge.

They handled the varnished wood steering tiller together for a moment, before his father asked, "Want to take the helm a bit while I go down below and fix up a snack?"

"Where do you want to go Dad?"

"Big Rock Point would be a nice heading for this wind." Tommy's father put his right hand over the boy's, and they turned the boat while he eased the jib sheet until the sail started to flutter, then tightened her up a half turn before cleating it again. "Can you see it?" Tommy stood up on his toes, "Yeah, I see it. Way up in front, its light is on."

"Keep her nose just off the port bow." It was an easy tack, and the sails were drawing nicely with the gentle breeze of the early night air. He made a quick look around and went below. The boy moved his small hands together firmly grasping the tiller; he could feel the rudder's pressure from the passing water beneath him and hear its whisper as it left the transoms wake. He was proud.

The father turned on the battery light over the small counter. With quick glances Tommy could see his father go about collecting stuff from the cooler and the drawer where his mother had kept the boat's forks and spoons and the dull knives that she let him get himself. He kept the boat's direction true.

"Do you want ham and cheese or cheese and ham?"

"Ham and cheese," smiling to the old question. They ate in silence, one on each side of the rudder's tiller, taking equal turns, sharing a can of ginger ale.

"You've got your mother's eyes. It's a nice evening for a sail."

"Yeah." The father had taught the boy about silence on the water and respect and the boy learned to hear without listening, and feel without touching, and see without looking. Passed the point now and heading northwest the sky became bright black with nature's countless lights. Dark, like it was before cities and electricity, and night was night and dark was threateningly long and lonesome. The hull of the little boat swept clean through the water, moving quicker now with a new wind, but still smooth without effort.

"Did you and mom sail a lot before me?"

"Some, but not enough. Mother liked to sail at night when it was clear with a moon, and the air was warm."

"Will we have a moon tonight?"

"In a while, look over there," the father pointed to a soft haze of light to the east.

"You can start to see its reflection on the water's horizon."

"I'll sail with you, dad—you won't be alone."

He reached over and scuffed the boy's blond hair then combed it back with his tough fingers. The father let the boy steer the boat while they located different stars, Venus and Mars and outlines of constellations. They each picked a star in the heavens and thought about it for a while. Tommy pointed to the sky to a polished sparkling diamond and with an excited whisper said, "See it—do you see it?" They focused their eyes of wonder to the dazzling star. "Is that her star?"

"Uh huh. The one left of Polaris." He crouched down and extended his arm and finger so Tommy could get a sight line to the right one. Tommy could feel his father's bristled cheek as they began to point at the bright star.

They gazed together, in their own separate ways, in their own silent prayers. The boy's eyes teared up.

"What's the matter?"

"I've been thinking dad."

"Yes Tommy?"

"Well … I've been thinking. "

"Well … that's good Tommy. Thinking is good. It's good to think." Tommy stood on his toes and gently pushed the tiller a few inches and felt the pressure of the rudder change and watched the bow move more to north. "Good job Tommy."

"I've been thinking dad."

"Yes … what have you been thinking about?'

"Well, I've been thinking, that maybe it is time … you know … it's about time I should be called … just Tom."

"Yes, it's about that time. "You are right. Just Tom." The father put his arm around Tom and pulled him close.

"We'll be fine dad … we'll be fine," as he wiped his nose and face on the sleeve of his shirt.

As the boat made its way north toward Good Hart, Tom got sleepy and put his legs up onto the lazarette while his dad grabbed a loose jacket and made a pillow for him in his lap. Then he took off his wool sweater and placed it over the boy as the wind grew brisk and adjusted the foresail without disturbing him. The cool wind felt good against his face, but he was not cold. He kept looking forward into the now dark horizonless Lake Michigan, looking for the Skillagalee Lighthouse on Gulls Island.

He sailed on into the night. He knew right where he was. He was on his lake, in his boat, with his son, Tom. He sailed on; he could not stop. He felt as though he could sail all night, taking big, long deep gulps of cool air until his chest would burst; and the salt on the edge of his lips tasted good.